"Are you looking for examples and concrete decision making? Well congratulations because it's in your hand. This book delivers the art of decision making in a unique, cool and straightforward way!"

Magnus Khysing,
Nordic Business Unit Head, SAP

"Thought Leadership involves not only a deep understanding of the trends that are shaping our environment but also, and importantly, it takes a willingness to take a stance, sometimes a brave decision to make for a leader. This book is unique in informing HOW such decisions should be made; it provides a great combination of novel insights and real life examples. And as for any good thought leadership, it is also is presented in a really engaging and actionable format. Deciding what to read or not to read is increasingly difficult in a world of information overload. Let me help you make that decision, read this book!"

Sophie Lambin,
Co-founder of Kite Global Advisors,
and former Director of Thought Leadership, PwC

Freestyle Decision Making

– Surfing the wave of information to get better results in life and business

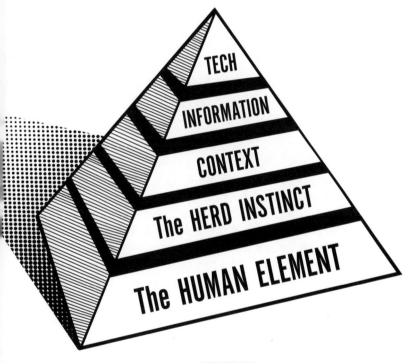

LONDON   MONTERREY
MADRID   SHANGHAI
MEXICO CITY   BOGOTA
NEW YORK   BUENOS AIRES
BARCELONA   SAN FRANCISCO

Published by
LID Publishing Ltd
1 Mercer Street,
Covent Garden,
London, WC2H 9QJ

31 West 34th Street, Suite 7004,
New York, NY 10001, US

info@lidpublishing.com
www.lidpublishing.com

A member of:

BPR
Business Publishers Roundtable
www.businesspublishersroundtable.com

Printed in Great Britain by TJ International
ISBN: 978-1-910649-07-7

Cover design: Laura Hawkins

To our children

The best way to run businesses and organizations is by making wise decisions – the same applies to our lives.

We make between 2,500 and 10,000 decisions per day - day after day, year after year - without giving much thought to how we go about it, much less to how we could do it better. Remarkable, wouldn't you say?

TABLE OF CONTENTS

FOREWORD

My attic is full of failed predictions. From the never used gym equipment to an embarrassingly expensive jacket worn only once and now gathering dust.

My attic is no exception. Wherever we look we see evidence of mankind's inability to make the right decisions about the future. From the amount of food thrown away in supermarkets to the fancy cars parked idly, unused, on the side of the street for a significant portion of their lives. We live in a society where even our long-term, high impact decisions are made spur-of-the-moment with no more evidence than some ethereal gut feeling.

Enter Dr and Dr Riabacke – on a mission to bring better decision making skills to the many people. Like a kind of IKEA for the mind, they take the intellectually heavy artillery from the ivory tower out to the streets and add a beat to it so we – all of us – can dance.

I first met Ari Riabacke in 2010 and was struck not by his academic credentials – although they are impressive – or his stellar intelligence but by his kindness and I do believe this is what sets him and his wife apart. The world is not short of PhD's and Professors who want to talk down to the little people and share some brilliant yet arcane insight on how bad we are at making decisions. Throw a tennis ball around the behavioural economics section in any bookstore and you're bound to hit a dozen in the first minute. Ari and Mona Riabacke are the antidote to these smug, predominantly male know-it-alls. The book you are about to flip or swipe through is testament to that. It is an upbeat, simple and useful guide to all of us who look at the dust-collecting paraphernalia in the attic or something more serious like a divorce certificate and go: "Why did I make such a bad decision?"

It makes me think about the people who pioneered modern medicine in the mid-1800's. Before that time, illness was treated with superstition and often connected to a sinful lifestyle. If you were ill, it was because you were poor, a woman, non-religious or simply just bad in the sense that you were not like the rest of us. Then came a series of brave individuals who challenged the status quo. I am thinking about people like Ignaz Semmelweiss who urged doctors in Austria to wash their hands between patients. They were treated as fools and had to preach a simple message of change – please wash your hands – for decades before it reached a breakthrough. The status quo doesn't like to lose its status so when we seek to change it, we inadvertently make enemies. Ari and Mona Riabacke are on a lifelong quest to change us into better decision makers. We come from a world where decisions were made sloppily in the last minute, often by serious looking men in boardrooms. In the new world, we all have to make decisions. About how to live, whom to marry, where to look for happiness and beyond. We are in the words of Charles Handy, another compassionate management thinker, condemned to freedom. So we need guidance, tools and ideas. I can think of no better people to guide us than Ari and Mona Riabacke and I look forward to the places they will take us to in this book and the many more to come from these brilliant, Nordic minds.

Magnus Lindkvist, Trendspotter and Futurologist

PREFACE

Never have we faced so many decision-demanding situations or so many options from which to choose. Every day, we make between 2,500 and 10,000 decisions and the tidal wave of information continues to rise. Decisions must be made at an ever-faster pace in an increasingly complex and fast-changing world. Dealing effectively with these challenges is not an easy task, particularly as it was only a "coffee break" ago, in terms of man's evolution, that we lived in caves.

So, to begin – what do we do when we make decisions? Most of us do as we always do or as everyone else is doing. We seldom consider how we go about making decisions, and above all, we don't mull over how we could do it better. A pity really, not least because arriving at good decisions is fundamentally essential to achieving success and the life that we want to live.

This is where this book, *Freestyle Decision Making,* comes into the picture. Adopting an explicit decision perspective is a winning approach for any business or organization that wants to increase its effectiveness and be successful in the ever-changing world in which we live today. It is the reason we have written this book – a book about how to make better decisions; a book about how decision problems emerge as decision opportunities; a book about the fact that it can be as easy as simply resolving to make decisions, to stop postponing decision making, to dare. We are profoundly enthusiastic about what we do, it is our calling and we live as we teach.

We are both Doctors of Philosophy, specialized in risk and decision analysis. Since 1999, we have been members of the Decide Research Group at Stockholm University, and spent periods of time abroad as guest researchers. Ari has been Head of Business Intelligence at Sweden's largest management and IT company, and Mona has worked as project manager for implementation projects within decision support.

Since 2011, we have managed Riabacke & Co (www.riabacke.se) – the decision experts, where we help businesses improve their decision making through advice-orientated consultation, education and workshops. Sometimes, for example, we may seek to create an understanding of how we humans function by giving speeches. Other times, we help identify the most important decisions and make sure that the decision making processes are in line with the company's established goals and strategies. Often, we help by providing structures to meet the preconditions necessary for better decision making.

Time after time, we see how many businesses and organizations are attempting to better their decision making by acquiring more technology. However, improving decision making requires more than just technology, which is also the main reason why the effectiveness of many such efforts falls short of envisioned hopes and expectations. Many times the most vital building block contributing to the resolution of decisions – the human, the so-called decision maker – is more or less lost and forgotten. Thus, a gap exists between available technology and people, as well as a knowledge shortage with respect to what it is that triggers people to act as they do when they make decisions. Our mission is to help reduce these shortages and gaps.

The concept, Pyramid of Decision Making, described in this book, rests on our joint research and experience within commerce and industry.

The Pyramid of Decision Making comprises five steps: the human element, the herd instinct, context, information, and tech (technology).

The steps rest upon one another, and without a solid foundation, the entire structure crumbles. In order to make better decisions, we must acquire greater knowledge about the pyramid's steps. We must acquire a better understanding of our fellow men, and ourselves, since it is still people – you and I – who make the decisions. We must begin at the foundation level, not at the pyramid's top.

We both hope and expect that the book's contents will awaken further thoughts and insights; create "aha!" experiences and, above all, increase understanding of how we human beings function in a world that has, in many ways, become alien to us.

Today, many of us seek and retrieve information faster than ever before. We race through cyberspace, jumping between articles, websites and other media. A bit here, a bit more there.

This is precisely why we have chosen to write this book in a format we believe will suit both the time and tempo of your lifestyle. It is a book that can be read whenever, wherever and however you want to: one page here, one page there – not a problem. In short, it's a book distinctly distant from traditional management literature and the never-read doctoral dissertations addressing this area. It is a book about the steps to wiser decisions – a book for you.

NO DECISION IS ALSO A DECISION

Many people are scared to death of making a wrong decision, which often leads to procrastination ad infinitum and yet another decision left to the hands of fate – which, in hindsight, is a choice (aka decision) they often come to regret.

Often, they justify the outcome with phrases like: "What a pity it became such a mess. Not my fault of course – I didn't do anything."

To make no decision is a decision in itself.

DECISIONS AND CHOICES – NON-STOP

Life is all about choices, about decisions, from beginning to end, 24/7.

1. Should we live in a big city or a small town, in a house or an apartment?

2. Who should I marry? When will we get divorced?

3. Meat, fish or salad for lunch?

4. Public or private school for the kids?

5. In which retirement fund should I place my money?

...and how would it have worked out if I had chosen differently? We'll never know. So stop worrying about the "what ifs".

TWO BIG DECISIONS

We have asked thousands of people to tell us which decisions, of all the decisions they have made in their lives, they consider the biggest and most important. Almost without fail, the answer reads: the person with whom I chose to spend my life and the purchase of my home. Amazingly often, people have also told us that, when it came to their choice of partner, "... it just happened."

When it comes to choosing one's partner, it appears we go about it in pretty much the same fashion as most other land mammals – which largely rely on scent – albeit, we like to think that we know what we're doing and, not least, why we're doing it.

On the other hand, when it comes to the purchase of a personal dwelling, we leave nothing to chance. This decision requires objective criteria and rigorous investigation: cost per square-foot, plumbing, lease, access to public transportation, quality of, and distance to, schools, ditto pre-schools and so forth. Here, not only must everything feel right – it must be right, case closed. We're talking money, serious money. Only a lunatic would consider completing on a purchase before carefully reading every item in the building inspector's report.

When we choose a partner, however, we do the "inspecting" ourselves. Moreover, it is not at all uncommon for such "inspections" to be carried out under the influence of alcohol. This is very rarely the case when it comes to the inspection of prospective homes.

Perhaps it's fortunate that certain "partnership inspections" take place in a bar, where our "inspection capacity" is not likely to be at its formidable best. Some couples may never have "discovered" each other without the romantic aid of subdued lighting and the courage-enhancing effect of one or another fortified beverage. Interestingly enough, research confirms that consuming even small amounts of alcohol makes other people appear significantly more attractive than when scrutinized sober.

Given that most people understand the importance of making wise decisions about matters that affect their personal economy, it might be worthwhile keeping in mind that by far *the most critical decision we make affecting our future economic status is the person with whom we choose to share our life.*

THE WORLD WILL NEVER BE NORMAL AGAIN

Certainty is something we human beings have sought through the ages. The ability to foresee the future, to look around the corner and far beyond the horizon, has always had appeal.

Everyone would like to know how it is going to be "later on" because we deeply wish – and are willing to go to extraordinary lengths – to avoid uncertainty in all its forms.

Today, however, the only thing we know with certainty is that uncertainty is here to stay, and that the future is no longer what it was perceived to be.

The future is hurtling towards us faster than ever before – in fact; it's already upon us. Moreover, it is full of uncertainty – of risk and, in the view of many, chaos.

The situations we experience are so different from what we've previously experienced; the information we struggle to digest so comprehensive, the risks we face so hard to foresee and avoid – harder than ever in a world where the improbable tends to occur with improbable frequency.

Times such as these demand active engagement; otherwise we will be swept in the wrong direction: backwards.

More than ever, we need to summon the guts it takes to act and make decisions. It is only then that we can pave the way towards security, and effectively address risk and uncertainty.

We create security by seeing opportunities where others see problems – by making decisions when others do not dare: we act, even though we, ourselves, are similarly uncertain about the outcome. We gain security through action.

In challenging times, the widely lauded character trait of being cautious is obviously often prevalent – we don't want to rock the boat, and we don't want to take any risks.

People who won't take risks are trying to preserve what they already have. People who take risks often wind up having more.

ARE MOST OF US BETTER THAN AVERAGE?

Most of us believe we are better than the average person at making decisions, it's human nature. In fact, we believe we are a little better than others when it comes to doing a great many things. Clearly, we're not run-of-the-mill average, but a little special, a little better.

Research shows that this innate over-confidence in ourselves and our own abilities asserts itself on many levels in our daily life. For example, the vast majority of us believe that we are more attractive and better company than we actually are (based on the responses of people who have met and spent time with us).

Most of us believe that we will repay miscellaneous loans faster than we can actually manage in reality. Consequently, many of us overlook the fact that the interest rate on any unpaid balance remaining after six months may be raised from, say, 6% to (an arguably usurious) 26% – after all, the loan will have been retired by then, right? We believe we have everything under control, even though others do not.

The same phenomenon afflicts new year exercise enthusiasts' intent on making good their solemn resolutions to work out three or four times per week, which naturally makes the purchase of an annual gym membership a sound investment. However, when the end of the year rolls around and the actual number of gym visits are totalled, the investment often appears as sound as a house of cards.

Thus, most of us believe we are somewhat better than most others when it comes to a great many things; not least, when it comes to making decisions. The additional example of 23-year-old male drivers is so classic that we cannot leave it un-noted: nearly all of them firmly contend that they are at least twice as proficient at driving as the population in general. It is the way most of us function.

It is also the reason why it is so painfully difficult for many of us to ask for help, or as our three-year-old son sums it up: **"I can do it – myself!"**

THE PYRAMID OF DECISION MAKING – IN BRIEF

The Human Element – Step 1 deals with how we human beings function when we make decisions. More specifically, it discusses how primal human behaviour such as sex drive, hunger, exhaustion and stress affect our decision making far more than well-polished reports and certified documentation.

The Herd Instinct – Step 2 reveals how the imprint of Neolithic herd behaviour impacts the decision making of 21st century human beings, both individually and in groups. It also reveals why making truly first-rate decisions requires both the presence, and serious consideration, of critical voices and opposing ideas.

Context – Step 3 addresses the often overlooked fact that no decision is made in a vacuum. For example, there is always a cultural context that envelopes the decision making process. No information is context-free. On the contrary, when we interpret information and make decisions, we are – to a great extent – steered by the context in which these tasks are being carried out.

Information – Step 4 deals with our decided tendency to spend enormous chunks of time and resources on becoming as well-informed as humanly possible, and how we often mix up the adjectives "more" and "good" when it comes to information. Just how much information can we effectively process in our already over-flooded brains? And why is half as much often twice as good?

Tech – Step 5 answers the question of why businesses so often fulfil only part of their initial vision when investing in various types of decision support. We then present a straightforward and simple solution to this persistent and very costly problem. Businesses, whether large or small, invest large sums in decision support systems. Unfortunately, these systems are all too often purchased and established without accounting for the most vital element of the system: the human, the so-called "decision maker", the person or people at the heart of the decision. Let us change this.

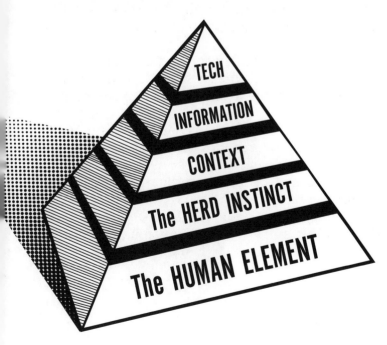

THE HUMAN ELEMENT

"Personally, I sway
wherever my
emotions lead"

Unknown

A STONE AGE MIND IN A CYBER WORLD

We live at a point and time in which the quantity of information, and the number of options available are overwhelming. In this virtual jungle of "possibilities" we can no longer be sure which choices are right, which path we should take. Should we rely on our common sense? Should we go with our gut feeling? Or maybe the best choice is to fall in line with what everyone else is doing and at least eliminate the risk of doing what everyone else is not doing?

The human brain has essentially remained unchanged for the past 30,000 years, and the response systems in our brains – systems that have been crucial for our survival and propagation – steer us more than all the Excel files, databases and highly polished reports we now snap up, like hungry ducklings in a well-stocked dam.

Our brains are version 1.0 and there is no new version in sight. This is a fact we must take seriously, and more to the point, a fact we must take into account.

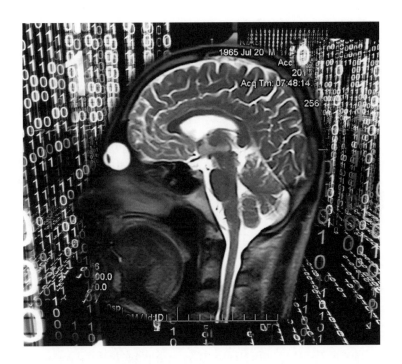

From the beginning of our existence, we human beings have been equipped with the instinctive will and inherent capacity to simplify issues when situations became too complex – hopelessly tangled by too many factors and options that were often contradictory. Consequently, we often act on emotional, rather than rational, grounds. Highly charged situations arise, for example, when we make emotional decisions before we are able to analyze situations in their entirety. This is precisely the challenge for many leaders today.

As a chief executive within the lumber industry put it: "The final, deciding puzzle piece to many heavy decisions is entirely emotional. In the end, it's the gut feeling that tips it in one direction or the other, no one can take in everything." Many people have wound up in precisely this sort of situation. We have turned a particularly troublesome situation inside out and finally emerged with a fully-fledged decision – for the simple reason that it felt right. This is completely ok. We are not alone. This is what we do, even though most of us don't want to admit it.

Often, this ability to simplify, to "feel" what is right via the memory or imprint of earlier successful choices (some instilled over thousands of years of evolution, and others through our own successes and failures) works to our advantage. We often know intuitively which choices are right and which are wrong.

There are many instances in which simplifying works extraordinarily well, but at other times, it can lead us to "feel wrong". Intuition, or gut feeling, also makes itself known when dealing with matters about which it has little, if any, experience. We intuitively feel we have been through something similar to what we are in the midst of experiencing, even though, actually, we have not. Sometimes, our intuitively "recollected" experiences turn out to be completely irrelevant to the ones we are experiencing in the here and now.

The world in which we live in today is changing at a faster pace than ever before, with the consequence that our "previous experiences" are sometimes not at all relevant to current, so-called modern, situations that we instinctively try to simplify and explain. The feelings, sensations, or the (sometimes completely subconscious) signals we pick up on, can be based on experiences that are not relevant to a current situation we are facing, in its modern context.

Some of our innate recognition functions have been critically important to our survival; for example, our ability to recognize – within a split-second – whether a situation poses a serious threat, and if so to flee or fight. But this remarkable ability doesn't always function quite as well in the world in which we live today. If we feel threatened by what someone, or some group, says or does at work, for example, it can lead us to act according to the "flee or fight" survival principle. Mildly put, resorting to either action (for example, an early exit or a "counterstrike") in such "pressured situations" is not going to earn us a promotion.

In such situations, we should instead train ourselves to be aware of, and control, our innate instincts and prevent our lightning-fast, primal fear-responses taking over. By taking a break and reflecting on a more conscious level before acting, our instinctive responses to threats are less likely to impact our decisions.

RATIONAL OR NOT?

How much of what goes on in our brains when we make decisions is made up of objective, logically sound deliberation – so-called rational thought – and how much is made up of something entirely different?

We believe that, at most, only one 1% of the thoughts running through our brains are neutral – which is to say, rational or objective. The rest, 99%, originate from sources that are hard for us to pin down. Clearly, it is high time we learned more about them, since it is principally these elusive sources that steer us.

Decision analysis rests on the precept that we are rational beings. It assumes that, when making a choice, we identify all available alternatives and carefully weigh up the probability and value of each until we have deduced which has the highest expected value (probability multiplied by value).

But most of the choices we make are based on grounds that are not rational, because, essentially, we are not logical entities. In order to act in accordance with the assumptions and rules of decision analysis, the emotionally responsive sections of our brains must be disconnected; a shut-down we human beings – for better or worse – find very hard to carry out.

THE HUMAN ELEMENT

When we speak about being rational, we often mean that we act – or at least try to act – with common sense, logically or, even more flatteringly, wisely.

Even the simplest everyday situations are too complex and information-intensive for our brains to process and must therefore be simplified.

Simply put, our natural decision making mechanisms operate by weighing the advantages and disadvantages (pros and cons) of various alternatives against one another and choosing a winner, if possible. Here, making a decision does not involve estimates of probability and the perceived value of a given alternative is often more a matter of a gut feeling rather than the result of a logically executed calculation.

When we talk to people about decision making, both in our private lives and in our research work, we often hear that they are weighed down by so-called "decision anxiety" – some more than others. Decision anxiety can be described as the sinking feeling we experience when we must make what we perceive to be a challenging decision .

Often, decision anxiety is grounded in the overwhelming quantity of information and alternative choices that are readily available to us in modern society and our consequent inability to make use of our "primitive" analysis in this realm. We constantly run into situations in which we are unable to see the full picture, much less pick the best alternative, regardless of what it is we're trying to decide. It could concern our choice of car, residence, career, partner, or the sort of life we wish to live.

In these situations, consider turning the task upside down. That is to say, as a first step towards making a decision, instead of racking our brains over the different alternatives and trying to identify the best, we could begin by coldly ascertaining which alternatives are the absolute worst, crossing them off the list, and continuing the decision process with the remaining alternatives.

Making use of the elimination method can often – right from the start – be of great help to us. By carrying out just this initial step we have already simplified the decision. There are now fewer alternatives, reducing the risk of making a truly awful decision, as the remaining alternatives do not include the very worst.

After completing this first step, some people may still feel they're not able to make a decision. In such an event, they can evaluate the remaining alternatives by making use of a more structured method.

MORE STRUCTURE

We can weigh the advantages and drawbacks among different alternatives using the criteria we consider most vital. For example, if I were to decide what lunch to order today from a take-out menu, my criteria might be: taste, price, nourishment, and how appetizing it's going to look and smell.

For other people, the list of vital criteria might very well differ. Thus, an important first step is to determine and list the criteria that strike you personally as being the most vital to the particular decision you're about to make.

With this accomplished, you can then compare the pros and cons of each alternative in meeting the criteria that you have listed. This way, the conditions for your decision will become clearer, and it will, for example, be more apparent whether or not you need further information regarding certain aspects.

For someone who enjoys working with numbers, an effective continuation would be to make use of a simple point system. For example, use the numbers one to three (where one represents the worst and three the best) to indicate just how good or bad you, personally, perceive each alternative in terms of how it meets each of your criteria. Observe that the points you assign are highly personal, that is to say, subjective. An example of this system is given here based on deciding what to order for lunch, as described above. If you consider that all the criteria you've established are of equal importance, simply total the points for each alternative to see which one comes out on top.

	Taste	Price	Nourishment	Appeal	Total
Hamburger	3	2	2	3	(10)
Carbonara	2	1	1	2	6
Shrimp salad	2	2	3	2	9

If the alternative that emerges as the winner after this calculation seems unreasonable, you have to consider the possibility that at least one of the criteria you listed carries more weight.

Should this prove to be the case, for example, that the taste of the meal is more important than its nourishment (no matter the dish selected), then a deeper fundamental analysis of the decision is called for.

If you're curious to learn more about this, you can read more in Mona's thesis, titled *A Prescriptive Approach to Eliciting Decision Information.*

Ps. If you have a yen to see Ari's thesis, it is called *Development of Elicitation Methods for Managerial Decision Support.*

DSV Report Series No. 12-008

Stockholm
University

A Prescriptive Approach to Eliciting Decision Information

Mona Riabacke

Doctoral Thesis in Computer and Systems Sciences at Stockholm University, Sweden 2012

THE LOGIC OF BEING INCONSISTENT

A phenomenon that has confused decision researchers over a long period of time is something called *intransitivity*, here meaning that we are not consistent (logical) in our way of making choices.

Consider the following example: suppose you prefer to eat a hamburger to pizza, and pizza to tacos. In order to be consistent in making your choice from this selection, you should prefer hamburgers to tacos. But is this the way it actually works? Well, sometimes yes, other times no. Thus, our "choosing behaviour" is not transitive.

Transitivity requires that if you prefer:

A over B and B over C, you should prefer A to C.

In the case of computers this principle works well, because they often perform in accordance with what has previously been determined. They are quintessential logical entities.

But what about us? No, the human brain is not a logical entity in that way. Not at all in fact. The human brain is a biological entity made up of several parts, or systems, including those where our feelings and the like have their say.

Psychologist Danny Oppenheimer of Princeton University proclaims that since the human brain has a limited reckoning capacity, and is often pressed for time when making decisions, it is only able to evaluate a limited number of attributes (criteria) for every alternative. Furthermore, he states that the brain uses a sort of "voting process", where various parts of the brain (with diverse preferences) may carry different weight on different occasions.

	First occasion	Second occasion	Third occasion
Part 1 of the brain (the criterion TASTE is most important)			
Part 2 of the brain (the criterion PRICE is most important)			
Part 3 of the brain (the criterion APPEAL is most important)			

Subsequently the outcomes of our decisions are determined by the part of the brain with the upper hand at the time. Therefore when we make a choice between similar alternatives, this type of voting process could certainly lead us to choose differently on different occasions. Often the time we have to make decisions is quite limited; therefore we don't always have the time to think of all the criteria that are vital to us.

In our hamburger, pizza and tacos example, this process can get us to choose pizza on one occasion, as the part of the brain that got to make this choice based the decision on the taste criterion. Whereas the next time, the choice may be made by a part of the brain that values the criterion of price, which, in turn, results in our making the intransitive choice of hamburger for lunch, and so on.

This could well explain why we humans do not always act consistently. It is an area with which decision researchers have been struggling for a considerable period of time, and sometimes makes it hard to predict human behaviour.

THE BRAIN'S TWO SYSTEMS

To a great degree, the make up and workings of our brains are still a mystery, but interest in so-called "neuro porn" is big, and knowledge in this area is constantly growing.

Within psychology, there has long been an interest in the different methods of human reasoning. Simply put, psychologists divide the brain into two systems, System One and System Two. System One is the more primitive system, where decisions are made quickly via an automatic response system expending a minimal amount of energy – often without time for or need of reflection. Belonging to this system are parts of the brain that steer, for example, our emotional life, our instincts and our fears. Here belong the remnants of the human brain's beginning, the so-called primitive brain – remnants that have, historically, helped us to survive. Whereas sophisticated thinking takes time, many people who have suddenly found themselves in danger, recount that they reacted instinctively, without thinking. Before there is a chance to think, this primitive system has already grasped that something is seriously wrong, that something dangerous is taking place, and decided on the best course of action – to flee or to stay and fight.

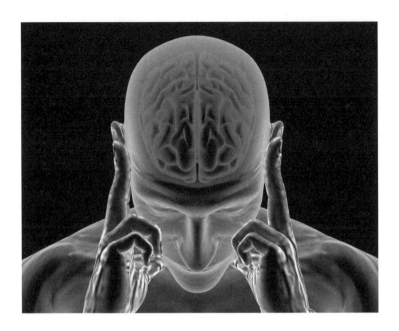

The fact that less strength and energy is required when using these parts of the brain can also be viewed as a necessity since this allows us to satisfy all the perfectly normal daily decisions we face. However, these same primitive brain characteristics can also cause us to make decisions that are less than satisfactory. Speed and efficiency, though impressive assets, make it possible for us to also react instinctively when faced with situations that require reflection and perhaps also a more rigorous analysis.

System Two houses the newer and more developed parts of the brain; parts that continue to develop until we reach 25 years of age. Here, we find our capacity to analyze, compare dimensions, make far-sighted plans, and think rationally – in short, our capacity to carry out more complex thinking.

As indicated above, this system is not fully developed in children. Hence, it is more difficult for them

THE HUMAN ELEMENT

to understand why, for example, we should hold off on eating sweets until after we've had dinner; particularly when such tempting treats are standing in plain view, and so on. The processing systems of these newer parts of the brain require more time and more energy, and tire more quickly. Moreover, they are easily disturbed by influences from the brain's primitive parts, often at a subconscious level.

In fact, we can suggest that the two systems compete with each other – that they push each other aside to some degree. This implies that when the more primitive parts of the brain launch their response to fear or sexual arousal, for example, the more advanced system doesn't perform especially well. These primitive mechanisms steer our decision making to a significantly higher degree than many of us are aware or understand. This lack of insight can cause us to make decisions that are significantly less sound when we are tired, frightened or emotionally compromised.

Most of us can attest that rational arguments have little effect on people head over heels in love. When we are in love, the emotional parts of the brain take over, suppressing the more analytical parts of our brain. In both our love and work lives this can lead to bad, or at least shortsighted, decisions, but it can also lead to the fulfillment of our dreams.

HALT – an acronym for hungry, angry, lonely, and tired – is a classic and effective mnemonic that can be of great help to us. When we find ourselves feeling one of these, we should refrain from making decisions.

The familiar phrase, "Let's sleep on it" often proves to be a more productive course of action than launching an emotionally charged "System One response" fuelled by our tiredness or hunger, for example.

WOULD YOU LIKE AN INJECTION OR TWO?

So, what course of action should we take, knowing that a great deal of the decision making process takes place on a subconscious level beyond our control?

Awareness of how we function makes it easier to be prepared. When we want to make a more aware decision, simple techniques to slow down our thought processes can prevent intuition from leading us astray. We can, for example, with conscious and deliberate intent, describe the feeling explicitly to ourselves by answering the question "what am I feeling and why?" By turning our emotions into words, we can prevent our subconscious from making decisions for us in situations we stand to gain by allowing our conscious system to gain control. Asking ourselves "why?" is a simple technique that can be used everywhere to connect with our rational system.

Does everyone have to contend with these challenges? Yes, including high-level decision makers. After all they are also human beings - no more, no less. Take, for example, Göran Stiernstedt, head of SKL (Swedish Association of Local Authorities and Regions) who was on the panel that, in 2009, decided to implement a nationwide vaccination programme against swine flu, using Pandemrix due to a predicted outbreak, which dominated media reports at the time. In November 2012, however, Stiernstedt publicly stated that he had hesitated to make the decision in 2009, but nevertheless urged the people of Sweden to get vaccinated as soon as possible.

In 2012, he was keen to know what had influenced his decision. If he were to address the very mechanisms of decision making, perhaps he would find that he was steered by the more primitive parts of his brain when making his choice in 2009.

In retrospect, he points to the fear of making a mistake as the prime force influencing the decision made in 2009. Narcolepsy, a brain disorder causing sudden sleep at inappropriate times, was a prominent side effect developed by hundreds of vaccinated children amongst others. In hindsight, knowing the serious side effects this vaccination caused, he is thoroughly convinced that the decision made in 2009 was wrong.

The total number of lives estimated to have been saved by the mass vaccination is disproportionate to the hundreds of lives it blighted – and all this at a cost of approximately 5 billion SEK (conservatively, around US $600million) in Sweden alone.

In an interview that took place on November 28, 2012 (via SVT – a Swedish television channel), Göran Stiernstedt said the following:

"We decision makers do not make only good decisions, we must be content if an overwhelming majority of our decisions are good, but we must learn from the others."

The biggest mistake was possibly that the decision was not revised when knowledge about swine flu increased, when the experts undisputedly knew more.

In general, once we have made a decision, we are reluctant to discard it, even with additional information and knowledge, which may have a significant bearing on the decision, as with this example of mass vaccination.

In other words, to change a decision that has already been made requires stronger arguments than the ones underpinning the original decision.

DIFFERENT TYPES OF DECISION MAKER

We are all different and there are many different ways of making decisions. For the sake of simplicity we can usefully categorize different approaches to decision making in order to aid understanding of this process. The following is one way of categorizing people into four different types of decision maker and is based on research on personality types and communication. Note that no personality type is better than any other, it is wholly dependent on the specific decision making situation.

Let's take a closer look at these four types of decision maker, what sort and style of communication works best for each of them and how to pitch ideas to them.

The Pragmatist focuses on the end result, likes to have control, and has zero tolerance of ineffective results or indecision. He or she takes care not to involve feelings. Decisions must be based on facts. Presentations and proposals to a pragmatist should be straightforward, objective and lead to the making of a well-considered, no-nonsense decision as soon as possible, one that will achieve the intended goal. Case closed.

The Visionary is creative during the decision making process and inclined to see the "big picture". He or she values intelligence, energy, fantasy and flexibility. Visionaries, in general, will gladly make use of unorthodox and innovative ways of making a decision, and wish to know, for example, how your products or services can help them achieve their goals. Boring presentations, with too much detail, are not welcome. When making a presentation or proposal to a visionary, you should be concise, maintain pace, let your energy flow and exploit the use of visual illustrations.

The Consensus Seeker wants to ensure that all involved in the decision making process are – to the greatest extent possible – happy with the result. He or she is sincere and cares very much about the feelings of others. The consensus seeker highly values relationships with co-workers, and will wish to see that the recommendation has apparent advantages for all the interested parties. Presentations and proposals for these individuals should be especially clear about the "positive" aspect and be well structured.

The Analyst requires a lot of information and reviews every conceivable aspect of a decision, wanting to know everything before he or she starts making one. The analyst examines every fact closely; intent on making sure it is correct. He or she wants to be furnished with plenty of detail, and to know why and how a decision is going to lead to the achievement of the goal. Analysts do not look favourably on surprises, and presentations to an analyst should be precise, systematic, logically and factually correct. The presentation for analysts should be prepared carefully, laying all the cards on the table, since the analyst will want to verify everything that has been stated.

THE HUMAN ELEMENT

MALE AND FEMALE

Many people wonder whether there is a difference between male and female decision making. Generalization is a risky practice with which we are seldom comfortable; after all, we are all individuals – unique and special – and history is full of erroneous gender stereotypes. But if we, nevertheless, dare to generalize a little (while keeping in mind that we are all inherently unique), we can make use of existing research that reveals clear differences.

Assertion: Having made a decision, men are not prone to having second thoughts. True or false?

In a study conducted by the US researchers Camerer and Montague, participants took part in a trust game. The game centred on making decisions about investing money and whether or not a player could rely on the opposing player. It revealed differences in the ways in which men and women reacted. By measuring the brain activity of the participants, the researchers were able to study how (and which) parts of the brain were activated during the course of the game.

The study revealed men's brain activity dropped off as soon as they had made their decision. While the brain activity of the women – in the part of the brain that controls worry and error detection – often remained unchanged after their decisions had been made.

The study is too small for any conclusions to be drawn. Nevertheless, it is a scientifically based indication that women appear to find it more of a strain than men to make a decision that involves social interaction, as in the case of the game used in this study.

Further confirmation that women are more affected by the social context (social setting) is provided by new research, which is a continuation of a classic study conducted at Stanford University (SU).

Let us begin with the original, classical SU study, in which men and women were given several calculation tasks to solve within a stated time. Each task was to calculate the sum of five two-digit numbers; for example, $12 + 34 + 22 + 73 + 41$.

Participants had five minutes to solve as many tasks as they could manage – and for every task they solved, they earned 50 cents. No difference was noted in the ability of the men versus the women to make the additions and, on average, each participant earned $5, reflecting an average completion rate of 10 tasks per participant.

Thereafter, they could choose to continue doing the tasks in a room with four other participants. But before they started, they had to choose between getting paid as before, per task-completed, or on the basis of "winner takes all". In this case, it meant that the person within each group who solved the

THE HUMAN ELEMENT

most tasks would take home all the money paid out for correct additions (roughly $25) while the rest would go home empty-handed. At this point, a big difference was noted between the male and female participants with respect to their choice of set-up:

Of the men, 73% wanted to go with the "winner takes all" option, while only 35% of the women chose this option.

Reflecting on the difference in the results observed, it was suggested that women are more risk-conscious and therefore choose the option with the better chance of payment, while men are more focused on winning and a "big bucks" pay-off.

With up to 73% of the men no better at performing the task than average, it is clear that some men have false confidence in their chances of winning.

We now come to the most interesting part. In the more recent study, which was almost identical to the first, one new step was quietly slipped in before the participants got to choose between the two payment alternatives.

This time, the participants were asked to answer one of two surveys:

• Half the group was asked to fill out a survey in which the questions related to their family situation and number of children.

• The other half was asked to fill out a survey containing a number of questions regarding their career plans.

A significant difference was noted in the women's subsequent choice of payment alternative, depending on which of the surveys they had completed. Of those participants who completed the career-related survey before choosing their method of payment, more women than men now chose the "winner takes all" option.

The conclusion drawn was that social context appears to have a greater influence on women than on men.

MEN ARE MORE COCKY BY NATURE

Overall, men are more prone than women to taking risks, both economically and physically, not least when an attractive member of the opposite sex is looking on. When it comes to making financial decisions, men are said to have a greater faith in their own capacity than women have in theirs. The article *Boys will be Boys: Gender, Overconfidence, and Common-Stock Investment*, published in 2001, firmly holds this to be the case.

Researchers were granted access to information about the common stock trading of 35,000 households and concluded that overly brave investors traded more, and gained less return on their stock transactions.

In short, the study revealed that men not only traded stocks more frequently than women (45% more) but also that single men traded less sensibly than married men and that married men, in turn, traded less sensibly than women in general.

Thus, the presence of women appeared to be a vital factor contributing to the achievement of sound trading in common stocks (or at least that was the connection made from the results of this study).

Moreover, further studies reveal that the participation of women in the various management and executive boards of companies is vital since businesses that only have men on their boards do not perform as well as those with boards made up of equal numbers of men and women.

"Children alike may well play best, but those poles apart will make play a quest."

This is vital to remember. Different personality types are good at doing different things, and thereby work to complement one another's knowledge and competences. So if you are the chief executive of an area or division, keep in mind that a well-performing group should comprise of both men and women, and above all of different personality types. Give extra thought and special attention to this if you see that a certain personality type is already dominant in your group or team.

When it comes to buying behaviour, it's said that men, to a great extent, make purchases based on short-sighted perspective – what they need just now or in the immediate-to-near future. Also, men focus more attention on pertinent product facts and information. By contrast, women tend to adopt a more far-sighted perspective when shopping.

Women are more often inclined to plan their purchases than men. Men often follow the buying decisions of others: "This buy has worked out well for others – chances are good that it will do the same for me." Women, on the other hand, often want to know the reason or reasons behind someone else's purchase: "There's no certainty that these reasons will apply to me. And yet, maybe I'll still want to buy the product."

Interestingly, women are said to be responsible for, or meaningfully influence, approximately 80% of all retail sales.

In other words, how women (as a target group) behave and make decisions is of great interest to all who work in sales and marketing, or at least it should be.

In the Swedish travel agency Fritidsresor's advertisement Days to Remember the attractive Danish actor Mads Mikkelsen is portrayed lying by a pool at one of the agency's hotels. At Fritidsresor, suspicions had begun to form that women tend to decide where a couple or a family will holiday. So it made its advertising appealing to women.

"Give us a 'hunk'!" was the bold instruction to the advertising firm, and the rest is history. Holidays flew off the shelf. Sales were 20% higher than for the same period the previous year. Women booked Fritidsresor's packages like never before, and men dreamed of becoming a little more like Mads.

SEX

Most of us agree there is no positive relationship between the consumption of alcohol and sensible decisions – no matter the specific beverage or subject to be decided. But what about our ability to reason and judge when we are sexually aroused?

Everyone understands, from a purely intellectual standpoint, that unprotected sex with strangers is not a good idea, particularly given the risks of unwanted pregnancy and sexually transmitted diseases. Therefore, it's fair to say that if the decision to have, or not have, unprotected sex solely depended on people's intellect there would be no problem. But, in reality, things work a bit differently.

In the US, at the renowned research facilities of MIT (Massachusetts Institute of Technology), a research team was able to study this more closely. Lo and behold, they found that:

We are surrounded by sexual stimuli, but we still have a very limited understanding of how this influences our decision making.

The study also arrived at insights applicable to stress, hunger, exhaustion and other physical states, states in which we often find ourselves when making decisions in our everyday lives.

In a nutshell: we react differently to the same situations and questions depending on the specific state in which we find ourselves.

In the MIT study, for example, the subjects had an entirely different moral perspective when they were not sexually aroused to when this primal instinct was very much awake and on the loose. They were very prim and proper in their answers to questions about their sexual experiences, preferences and desires when in a non-aroused state, but there was a pronounced shift in their responses, when in a state of sexual arousal.

In the latter state, they were significantly more open to suggestions which they had previously dismissed or even condemned. The study observed and duly noted that: "The participants' moral perspectives had changed considerably."

In the aroused state, for example, they were often willing to have a third party join in their "love-making".

How is it, for example, that someone who could never think of making a single decision without having first checked the accuracy of every dot and dash in an Excel file, will choose to have sex with a colleague at a Christmas party ... despite the fact that such behaviour is traditionally ridiculed as being anything but helpful to the interests of business or the group dynamic in the long-run?

STRESS, HUNGER AND FATIGUE

A study of more than 1,150 requests submitted by prisoners, seeking to be pardoned or have the length of their sentences reduced, was conducted. The attorneys and review panels which handled these petitions were naturally not informed as to the precise purpose of the research (had they been told, the chances are they would have taken pains to sharpen their performance).

As it was, the study revealed that the probability of being granted a pardon or a reduced sentence was approximately 65% when the proceedings began in the morning, only to sink to almost nil before the advent of the first coffee break. Immediately following this break, the probability of a favorable outcome once again rose to the 65% level, only to once again sink towards nil before it was time for lunch.

You no doubt have more than just an inkling about what happened to the probability after lunch – and yes, 65% -> 0% again.

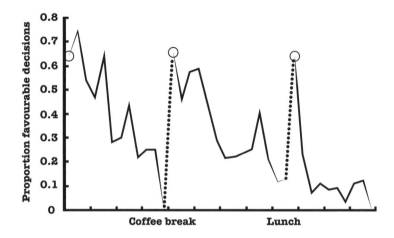

When a person is tired, bored, and has low blood sugar levels, it is always easier to say "no" – to choose the simplest "solution" and follow the well-trodden path instead of striving to find a better one: is this the way to go, or is there a better alternative?

For example at the end of a surgical shift, when a brain surgeon has concentrated hard for a long time, they are not likely to come up with the smartest solutions even if they have a strong tendency to think they do. So doesn't it seem a little strange that brain surgeons often believe they come up with the smartest solutions towards the end of their surgical shifts, when in all probability this is not likely to be the case?

THE HUMAN ELEMENT

DO YOU REMEMBER WHAT YOU REMEMBER?

Retrieving a memory is not like retrieving a record of funds paid out from a bank account, where the exact status and purpose of transactions are documented. No, retrieving a memory provides us, instead, with a notoriously subjective "as I recall it, just now" memory story.

We hear what we want to hear; we see what we want to see – and the same applies to our memories – we remember what we want to remember.

When we don't really remember, our brains automatically fill in the gaps and we recall, happily enough, what suits us. Our memory is like a large jar of candy into which we dip when it fits with our aims and motives.

Who hasn't sat in a meeting and discussed what was said in the previous meeting, only to be dismayed by the realization that we remember things differently from colleagues. Sometimes it feels as if we attended different meetings. It is amazing how often we recall things that support or favour our standpoint; scenarios that are to our advantage, that promote our aims or interests. It is rarely the other way around. We hardly ever remember only the details that favour other parties, and completely blank out whatever is beneficial to us and/or supports our agenda.

As unique individuals, we quite simply remember events, from our own personal perspectives. We take in and sometimes enhance different elements of the scenario. In truth, we have forgotten most of what happened at the last meeting, but now we have refreshed our memory so that it matches our own agenda, more-or-less perfectly.

Assertion: "Memory can be likened to a warehouse in the brain in which we store material we can later retrieve for use as needed. Sometimes, however, we lose some of the stored material and say that we have forgotten."

In a US study, 82% of the subject group agreed with the assertion made above. However, our memories cannot be likened to a bank statement that provides us with precise details of account transactions. Memory is a subjective picture of how we remember things from the past.

When people are asked, for example, to remember a fine summer's day at the beach, most can picture lying comfortably on the sand, perhaps how their children played with buckets and spades and which, if any, of their friends were also there. In reality, we haven't recalled this image at all, it has been actively constructed in our minds. Only 10% of what we see comes to us through our eyes, the rest takes form somewhere in our brains. It is also interesting to learn that every time we root up a memory, we erode it, as new nerve connections are created. The brain rebuilds the memory, so that we can remember.

In recalling a memory, our memory image is thereby changed. As more time passes from when we experienced something, the greater the risk that we have reconstructed it in our memory. Many people have a tendency to remember the good times and let the trying times sink to the darkest depths of their memory banks. Every time we remember an event, certain details are liable to fall away and others to climb aboard. Our memories thus change over time, whether we wish it or not.

An example of how this memory change phenomenon can be particularly problematic is the sworn testimony of witnesses during a trial. Which details are fact and which are not? The witness can be honestly and fully convinced that the scenario he or she describes in court is exactly how it happened, but time and repetition of the story can have combined to alter it.

When we find it almost impossible to remember what another person claims to remember vividly, we sometimes accuse each other of lying. But often no conscious distortion of reality has taken place. The difference could well result from inevitable changes, wrought over time, in each party's unique memory of the situation, meeting or event.

One way of avoiding disputes in the workplace is to take minutes at meetings and document what is said and decided. Taking note of who has been asked to do what, when these tasks are to be done, the available resources, and so on. If we don't do this, as surely as day follows night, it is guaranteed that participants will not remember everything precisely as it was said and done and we will not get done everything that was discussed.

HEURISTICS AND BIASES

By the early 1970s, Nobel laureate Daniel Kahneman and Amos Tversky – two of the legends within decision research, who pioneered the combining of psychology and economics in their studies – had already revealed that we, purportedly rational, human beings make use of so-called heuristics ("rules of thumb") to support our decision making.

The development of these rules of thumb is achieved by the repetitive process of successful choices, either through evolutionary selection, where certain behaviours have played out well, or through knowledge gained by trial-and-error in everyday life. Kahneman and Tversky clarified, with simple examples, how these rules led to systematic errors (biases) when we made evaluations, choices and decisions. Over the years, other researchers have identified a great many heuristics, and these discoveries can help us when we're about to make a mistake "automatically".

Let's take an example:

Our recollection of something can vary a little, depending on the availability of this information in our brain. This is called *the availability heuristic.*

I.   How many English words can you think of that have the letter "n" as the word's penultimate letter? (_ _ _ _ n _)

Perhaps not many – not straight off the bat. Let's try another question:

II.   How many English words can you think of that have the ending "ing"? (_ _ _ _ i n g)

You surely noticed that it is considerably easier to come up with words such as jogging, flying and so on, when we are given the full "ing" ending rather than the penultimate "n". The fact is that the total number of English words with "n" as the penultimate letter (without a preceding "i" and a finishing "g"), is considerably greater than those ending with "ing". And yet, despite this, the "n-only" words are clearly much harder to extract from our memory bank than the "ing" words.

A similar bias, called *the conjunction fallacy*, occurs when people believe that events A and B are more likely to take place than event A alone. Here again, Kahneman and Tversky helpfully provide us with a classic example:

The probability of an atomic war being launched by terrorists is greater than the probability of an atomic war starting.

In other words, people believe that:

A (the start of an atomic war) + **B** (by terrorists)

is more probable than

A (the start of an atomic war)

– which is clearly not the case.

A scenario can never be more probable simply because it has been made specific or "reinforced" by detail – quite the contrary. The challenge in overcoming this mind trap rests in the fact that most of us automatically see what has been described in more detail as being more probable. We can more easily relate to and understand it in this form, particularly if this detail takes advantage of existing preconceptions.

WHICH LINE IS LONGER?

Most of you didn't need many seconds – possibly not even one – to see and understand that they are equal in length.

I have seen this classical optical illusion 1,000 times before: as stated, they are equal in length.

But now we are a little further into the 21st century, the lines are no longer equal in length. The second line is 10% longer than the first one. A little strange, no?

How has this come about? How is it that two lines that have been of equal length since time immemorial can, all of a sudden, be different lengths?

What we "know" and have seen before is not always what it appears to be. The arrows are no longer the same length as each other; times have changed.

Future knowledge is about being able to see around corners, about thinking outside the bounds of what has already been thought – to understand and accept that even arrows of this sort can be different in length. We realize that this is asking a great deal, but we mean only well – the very best.

We must relearn. We must strive and strain not to think as we have always thought, or as others are always thinking.

To think as everyone else is thinking ensures, at best, that we advance as far as they do – but not one step further.

SOMETIMES
THE HEART HAS
A HARD TIME
ACCEPTING
WHAT THE MIND
ALREADY KNOWS.

SUMMARIZING TIPS

- Feelings come upon us more quickly than thoughts and steer us whether or not we wish it – be alert!

- By being more aware of the more primitive parts of the brain and their reactions, we can learn to control them better in situations in which we need to act more rationally.

- When we are frightened, tired, hungry or sexually aroused it is more difficult to access the brain's more analytically advanced systems. Try to be in a balanced state when you make decisions.

- Gut feelings or intuition are often appropriate for swift decision making. When making vital decisions you should be on your guard, because intuition has been known to make itself felt in matters about which it has little or no understanding of.

- When you are faced with decision anxiety, it may help to begin by sifting out the worst alternatives, and selecting an option from among those that remain. If this is not sufficient, you can structure your options further.

THE HERD INSTINCT

When everybody
thinks alike, nobody
thinks very much.

RECOGNIZING THE PATHS WE HAVE ALWAYS TAKEN

A round 100 years ago, in the jungles of Guyana, the naturalist William Baker came across a large ant colony that appeared to be lost.

The ants wandered around and around in a circle that was more than 100 metres in diameter, and eventually, over time, they all dropped dead – one by one.

None of the ants wandered off, none were struck by the thought that perhaps they should shift their route to the right or left, or perhaps simply march straight ahead?

Instead, they followed slavishly behind their compatriots who appeared to know where they were going, which turned out to be somewhat untrue.

THE HERD INSTINCT

We humans essentially encounter the same phenomenon when we lack the necessary backbone and will to veer off the beaten track and take a path other than the one that has been laid out for us; to step away from the traditional ways of making decisions in corporations and organizations, or to live our own lives.

We frequently act on information we believe others have; others, who in turn, are acting on information they believe others have, and so on. This chain is what constitutes the so-called market.

The market is not steered by rational thinking, but rather by feelings and the declaration of self-proclaimed prophets (or, as we in the banking and finance sector commonly call them, qualified guesses).

The overall health of the 21st century's financial sector would be notably improved by blending in a little new, healthy blood among its economists (today, packaged and sold 13 for a dozen). Why not add people such as psychologists and behavioural researchers to this extraordinarily homogenous group?

It would provide a comprehensive perspective of group psychology, on a national and global level.

WHERE ONE LEADS, OTHERS FOLLOW

The more people there are who do something in a certain way, the more people there will be who follow their lead. This is called *social proof*. As it happens, social proof is often confused with social conformity. But social proof does not denote desiring to be like others, but rather a technique to which we often resort when we don't know how to act in a certain situation. We sneak a look at what others are doing – and then do the same.

The determining force or motivation, then, is that we believe everyone else knows something that we've either missed or for some other reason haven't got a grip on.

Let's take a closer look at a few examples. We'll begin with one of the sillier ones: the so-called "canned laughter" used in TV programmes.

How many people find canned laughter amusing? Raise your hands! No one? Remarkable. Then why in heaven's name do we add it when no living person finds it amusing?

Ok – well, here's how it works. Research has quite definitively established that the programmed laughter on TV shows encourages us to laugh both harder and longer. This is the simple and self-evident reason why TV bosses remain intractable when it comes to the use of this entertainment enhancer, despite the fact that certain actors refuse to take part in programmes that use canned laughter. These anonymous TV broadcasting and production executives, not to mention sponsors, who probably do not find canned laughter funny themselves, blindly rely on research findings that unequivocally state that viewers laugh more when a little extra laughter is inserted here and there, and experience the programme as being more entertaining.

This same research has also revealed that the use of canned laughter is particularly effective when the joke level is second rate.

So why do we laugh more? Are we bonkers – or what? The answer is that we quickly develop a sense of the program's hilarity via the artificial laughter used – even though we don't like canned laughter, and even though we know there is someone sitting in a control room pushing the "laugh-button".

A study conducted by Stanley Milgram in 1968 is another example of how other people's behaviour affects how we act. When social psychologists placed a person on a street corner and had that person stare up at the sky, only 4% of the people passing by joined in that activity. In the next stage of the study, 15 people were placed on the street corner, heads thrown back staring up at the sky – and suddenly, 40% of the passers-by stopped, of whom 90% joined in the group's behaviour and also stared up at the sky. Needless to say, there was nothing unusual to look at.

The behaviour of others influences us to an astonishing extent, and awareness of this influence can be exploited in various areas, such as in politics (which party to support), the environmental agenda, eradicating racism, and so forth. But most commonly, such awareness is used to extract money from us; for example, via sale campaigns aimed at getting us to buy certain products. Imitating others is a characteristic that lies deeply rooted within all of us. It's the way we learn as small children and most of us – to one degree or another – continue to imitate even as adults.

Since 95% of all people are imitators and only 5% are initiative-takers, we are far more influenced by the actions of other people than by documented proof or rational arguments.

From a historical perspective, this inherent characteristic of following the majority has helped us make fewer mistakes. And often, this is still the right thing to do; above all, when we don't want to risk making a mistake and end up standing alone.

We witness daily proof of this behaviour when we see people choose a busy restaurant, which appears full, rather than one that has ample available seating. We've also observed how a long queue "inexplicably" attracts, rather than discourages, night club visitors, and how a person who is eagerly sought after by many is soon being eagerly sought by many more.

Curiously enough, when it comes to taking responsible action as, for example, when we see someone in acute distress, the opposite often applies. It has been proven that the fewer people observe a person in distress, the more likely it is that one of them will try to help.

A vicious crime that stirred up a great deal of interest in the US, took place in March 1964 on a dark street in the mostly residential New York City borough of Queens, where a woman named Catherine Genovese was brutally murdered. She had been sexually assaulted and stabbed to death in the black of night, on her way home from work. It turned out that Catherine's murder had not gone unseen – far from it. There were 38 witnesses to the young woman's terrifying ordeal and screams for help. The attack dragged on for more than half-an-hour – but no one intervened or even called the police until after she lay dead.

Since then, a series of studies has laid waste to the idea of "safety in numbers". In one such study, conducted in 1968, it was statistically determined that a person who appeared to be having an epileptic fit, received help 85% of the time providing there was only one person close by. If five people were in proximity, the probability of getting help dropped to 31%.

What does this mean, or imply, about us as individuals in the society in which we live? And what's the effect on the decision making of businesses?

It means that we tend to spread responsibility and also that the greater the number of people involved in a troublesome situation, the more we try to avoid taking any responsibility.

"Sounds good, let's do that!" But it later unfolds that nobody was assigned to do it and nobody took responsibility for making sure it was done.

The "someone else will take care of it" syndrome has become so widespread that soon there will be no "someone else" left.

When a decision is going to be made there must always be someone who is ultimately responsible – that is our unwavering experience. Assigning a "responsible someone" to make sure that appropriate measures are taken after the decision is made is just as important as making the decision.

THE HERD INSTINCT

C.R.I.T.I.C(al) DECISIONS

If you want things to happen and decisions to be made (on time), there's a need for guidelines and an explicit action plan for how decisions are to be made. The plan doesn't need to be advanced, but believe us – it's needed.

An action plan needs to be drawn up and, in one way or another, documented. Once we have an action plan for decision making, it is less likely that we will suffer from the "someone else will do it" syndrome, whereby nothing is decided by anyone.

An action plan can be outlined in many different ways, and it's important to consider where action is needed, in order for decisions to be made. A simple place to start out from is to make it a rule that decisions made are CRITIC(al):

Criteria – which criteria (for example, cost, time, quality) should underpin the decision and whether some are more important than others.

Responsibility – who is responsible for assuring the decision is made?

Information – what type of information is required in order to make the decision?

Time limit – what is the time limit for making the decision?

Intent – why the decision is being made, the intent (sometimes, but not always, obvious; you may need to discuss the important criteria first)?

Contingencies – is the decision contingent on other decisions before it can be made?

If you make several decisions that are similar, a so-called "category of decisions", it's wise to create a distinct decision process expressly for each category. It will initially take more time, but in the long run, it will save time. It's unnecessary to re-invent the wheel every time.

For our important decisions and those we make repeatedly, it's advantageous to have decision processes in place. They don't have to be advanced and they are highly individual – depending on such things as core business, context, employees, and aim. Then, everyone knows who is responsible for the decision making, the important criteria to evaluate possible alternatives against, the timeframe available and the basis on which decisions should be made (among other things), in order to achieve the quality needed. Having decision processes in place create the conditions for people across the organization, from novices to seniors, to make decisions better and faster.

Last but not least, it is also important to have an action plan for *the execution of what has been decided.* Often we make a decision but we do not act on it so it is important that as we structure the decision making itself, we also remember to structure the execution of the decision (if we decide to go ahead and do something). Optimally, we should always debrief the process as a very last step before it's iterated again to constantly improve and adapt to possible changed circumstances (this last step is important yet often forgotten).

CONFORMING

Social proof has a strong influence when uncertainty sets in, for example, when we have too little or too much information, or when we enter a state of paralysis because we sub-consciously assume that, with so many people present, someone else is likely to act.

Another factor that triggers the same mechanisms, and influences our decision making, is the feeling of kinship or similarity with other people. When others who appear to be very like us do something, we tend, to an amazing extent, to do the same thing.

The vast majority of us wish to safeguard the environment – which is good. But if we find a "thoughtful" sign in a hotel bathroom that poses: "The reuse of towels is environmentally friendly", the influence of this piece of information is nowhere near as influential as if we are informed that many of the hotel's other guests, up to 90%, choose to reuse the towels.

As we are strongly inclined to do what others are doing, no matter whether it's good or bad; even relatively minor commonalities are often sufficient to create a feeling of fellowship and trust.

Examples of small common factors that can influence our decision making include having grown up in the same area; having a mutual acquaintance; or even something as trivial as sharing the same birth month or astrological sign. Salespeople have long made use of the "commonality" technique, real commonalities or fabricated ones, in order to increase sales with the help of slogans like: "The most sold!", "Fastest-growing in the market", and "Eight out of 10 people prefer..." In the corporate world, customer word of mouth, contacts and references are extremely important – after all, the more people who buy something, the more people follow suit.

In a study focused on "fundraising" in the vicinity of a university, it was found that the sum of money donated more than doubled where the people who helped raise money presented themselves as being students, just like the young people they were canvassing. The same technique is successfully applied when petitions are presented to potential supporters with a list that includes the signatures of friends and neighbours.

WHEN WE MAKE "HERD DECISIONS"

Often, groups are too large to be effective in their decision making and may need to reduce their membership to reach a viable size. Half as many can very well be twice as good. In addition to being large and unwieldy, a group's ineffectiveness in decision making often stems from being too homogenous.

In homogenous groups a phenomenon known as "groupthink" has a tendency to flourish. When everyone thinks alike, critical voices are notable by their absence, and an almost tangible feeling of the group's superiority to others grows stronger than the will to make truly good decisions. In such cases, there are guaranteed serious flaws, and hence, great possibilities for improvement as well.

Inflated confidence or belief in one's own intrinsic worth, the feeling of belonging to an invincible group, in combination with the human tendency to essentially see things and act in the same way as the others in the group, creates an atmosphere in which ideas that don't fit with the group's perspective are regarded as threats.

The restrictions and forbidden viewpoints dictated by the group's narrow vision grow to the point that they undermine decision making. Options and possibilities become limited.

In order to avoid such problems, it is important to take measures that safeguard the continuous flow of new ideas and new blood into the organization.

Procedures that stipulate how decisions are made should also be put in place, and a climate developed that values and encourages employees to think laterally and creatively, not according to tradition.

But how should a group decision be made, where the group's collective wisdom must be captured and converted to action?

In an ideal world, the values (input) of each group member should be elicited in an objective manner; each should be asked what they think, how they reason and what they believe about the chances, risks, alternatives and so on.

If the group has been correctly, or better still, ideally selected, then every member has something unique to contribute. We won't stipulate what this might be but keep in mind that if there are two members who think and reason in the same way about everything, then they are one too many. Essentially, there is something called *confirmation bias*, meaning that when we look upon "the world" (look for information etc) we both consciously and sub-consciously see things that confirm our views, previous knowledge etc and sort out that which doesn't. We confirm what we know or think we know. We are also drawn to people like ourselves, which only enhances this tendency as we see the same thing. So, when we ask someone for advice, we shouldn't ask those

THE HERD INSTINCT

who we almost know what they will tell us but those who won't, provided we want a more objective view of course!

To elicit what each member thinks, reasons, prefers or suggests effectively, it is important to come up with a way of reducing the risk of members being influenced by the answers of their peers in the group, which is not that easy. As discussed, it is each member's independent, unique knowledge that often makes group decisions better than the decision of a single individual.

The group can surely come up with many good ideas, but the rewards of collective wisdom in its purest form are seldom reaped if group members have been influenced by one another – which is generally the case.

In order to avoid an influential boss or an informal leader setting the agenda for how and what group members should think and reason – what is right and what is wrong – it's a good idea to bring in outside help to elicit the input of individual members. Often, an entirely different set of suggestions come out of meetings and workshops when the boss is elsewhere.

Let's get you acquainted with two classic examples of group work that have been carried out along the lines suggested above, wherein each individual contribution carries equal weight, and where members have not influenced one another.

I. In 1968, the US submarine Scorpion vanished without a trace, in the North Atlantic. Months of searching for it heralded no result. The search area was concentrated within a circular expanse measuring 20 nautical miles in diameter – its location was based on the only clue the searchers had to go on: the vessel's last radio signal.

A naval officer by the name of John Craven came up with the idea, highly unconventional at the time, of putting together what is now referred to as a multidisciplinary group. In this case, the group comprised of people contributing expertise from different fields and included psychologists, meteorologists, naval officers, and statisticians. All were given access to the same information and their respective input as to where the submarine was likely to be located was elicited. Once the material submitted by the experts – who had worked independently without having communicated with one another – was put together, the submarine was located with uncanny precision, only a few hundred metres from the spot to which the collective guess had pointed.

II. On an autumn day in 1906, the British scientist Francis Galton was walking through a farmer's market when he came upon a 'guess the weight' contest. The subject of this contest was a large ox, and estimates of the net weight of its carcass, butchered and packed were collected. Approximately 800 people, many of whom were either farmers or butchers (experts), guessed (some soundly, some wildly). The estimates of the experts were blended in with guesses made by enthusiastic amateurs who had not the slightest knowledge of farm animal weights.

Galton was curious to know what the average of the submitted weight guesses would be, He presumed that, by combining the guesses from qualified experts with those made by rank amateurs, the resulting average would wind up way off the mark.

When all was over and done, he gathered the information he needed, and to his great surprise, he discovered that the calculated average of all guesses came to 1,197 lbs. The ox, butchered and packed, weighed 1,198 lbs!

The point being made here is that viewpoints or opinions coming from a wide spectrum of competence, both high and low, are needed and are of intrinsic value. A group comprising only of experts in the example above would probably not have arrived at an average guess as near to the precise mark. The same also applies, with an even greater degree of probability, to the counter side; that is to say if a group of experts were substituted with a group of low-competence amateurs.

Examples of more advanced versions of this phenomenon today are founded on the same principles. These are the establishment of various types of centres of excellence at companies, which aim to assemble knowledge and competence, along with different types of evaluation and perspective. Within the field of decision support, for example, BICCs (Business Intelligence Competency Centres) are often set up.

NEVER LET THE FEAR OF FAILURE KEEP YOU FROM PLAYING THE GAME

"I've missed more than 9,000 shots in my career. I've lost almost 300 games – 26 times I've had the confidence to take the deciding shot and missed. I have failed time after time in my life and that's why I have succeeded."

Michael Jordan

In Sweden today, ensuring nothing goes wrong has almost become more important than getting it right. The most important thing is not to fail; often, it seems we'd rather die than stand there with the shame of failure.

What will everyone think if I fail? What will the neighbours say? Will we have any friends left? Not to mention the situation at work ... Oh no – better to stay on the safe side. It's not worth the risk – and it would probably never have worked out anyway.

All that is exciting, all that is different, all that makes us develop begins precisely where safety comes to an end and uncertainty begins, where possibilities spire up on the horizon, where we are no longer following someone else's footsteps – not even walking side by side.

It is better to have tried and failed than not tried at all. We are often restrained from making decisions that are unconventional, different and so on, but the world moves at such a fast pace that things are not what they have been, and we need to make decisions faster and dare to try new things in order to keep up and adapt to the future. Trying new things include failures as well.

We may become disappointed if we try and don't succeed, but we are doomed to fail if we never even try.

FREAK OUT DUDE!

The challenge is not that everyone makes wrong decisions, the challenge is that everyone makes the "right decisions". Everyone does the same because everyone has gone to the same schools, learned to reason along the same lines. Everyone has the same interests, and everyone wants to be admired by everyone else. Everyone wishes to be what he or she believes everyone else wishes to be.

There are far too few people who are themselves.

Imagine that you are going to employ a staff member. Don't choose a person who thinks precisely the same way you do. Don't choose a person who appears to be completely right – a person who strikes you as just the sort of employee you had in mind.

Instead, when you come across a person who is the opposite of what you had in mind, a person who has not gone to the same schools as you and your colleagues, does not speak the same language, a person with whom you might not click immediately, a person, moreover, who doesn't say things you wish to hear – this might be the person you are looking for, or at least, should be looking for.

Don't pour over other people's job ads, you'll find they're all the same, because all those recruiters placing job ads before you had also poured over earlier ads and then created theirs similarly.

Management guru Tom Peters, along with Kevin Roberts, CEO of a well-established PR bureau, have both publicly expounded the vital importance of employing "freaks".

Peters brought to light, among other items, the following vital points in a presentation:

• When interesting things happen, they will have been done by a freak.

• We need freaks. Especially in freaky times.

• Surrounding yourself with freaks makes you seem somewhat freakier, which is important because ... we need freaks.

• Freaks are the only (only) ones who make it into the history books!

Or as Daniel Pink, previously Al Gore's speechwriter, puts it:

"Talking with only the usual suspects can become an echo chamber."

CREATE AN "OK TO MAKE A MISTAKE" ATMOSPHERE

In Stanford Professor Robert Sutton's book *Weird Ideas That Work*, it is revealed that when Time Warner CEO Steven Ross first started up MTV, he intended to fire people who never made mistakes, in order to break traditional patterns that people are normally inclined to follow.

Rumour also has it that, at one point in its history, Microsoft had a policy of waiting until people had experienced at least one major public failure before promoting them.

Are these stories true? We don't know, but they are so good it's not worth the risk of verifying them.

Never forget that if we don't dare to make mistakes, we rule out the possibility of doing things right.

WHATEVER YOU THINK — THINK THE REVERSE.

SUMMARIZING TIPS

- We often base our actions on the assumption that others have information or knowledge that we lack, without giving much thought as to whether it's actually the case. Have more faith in yourself!

- Bear in mind our tendency to side-step responsibility, which goes a long way to explain why the more people are involved in a challenging situation (such as an accident) the less responsibility we feel or take as individuals.

- If we find it difficult to make and/or carry out decisions, the mnemonic C.R.I.T.I.C(al) is a hot tip and a good start to taking a structured approach to tackling decisions proactively.

- For our important decisions and those we make repeatedly, taking the time to set up a distinct structure for processing such decisions, a decision process, is a sound investment of time.

- To ensure that a group makes better decisions than individuals, it is of utmost importance that:

- all participants are there for a distinct reason, and each has agreed to and is comfortable in his or her role.

- all participants complement one another in terms of their knowledge.

- the atmosphere within the group is open to constructive criticism.

- everyone is given the chance to express his or her knowledge before the group discusses the matter collectively in order to prevent individuals being influenced by others or simply following the crowd.

Step 3 of the Pyramid of Decision Making

CONTEXT

No decision takes place
in a vacuum — there is
always a context.

WHAT YOU SEE DEPENDS ON ITS CONTEXT

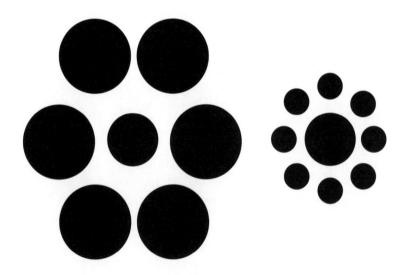

CONTEXT

This optical illusion carried out with circles is a good example of how our eyes can deceive us; more specifically, that the context in which we view something can lead us to perceive it differently.

In this case, both centre dots are identical in size, but we are deceived by a phenomenon called the "Ebbinghaus-illusion". What we see is a "picture" put together by the visual cortex located in the rear-most area of the brain, the result is that not all of us experience the size of the centre dots as being identical.

A percentage of us think there is a big difference in the size of the centre dots, while others estimate that although there is certainly a difference in their sizes, it's not all that profound.

Only about 10% of what we "see" enters through our eyes – the remaining 90% comes from other sources, influenced by previous experiences and knowledge, as well as our motivations and expectations.

This is one of the key reasons why we neither see nor experience the things we look at in exactly the same way as others, despite having witnessed an identical scene or event.

THE RIGHT PERSON IN THE WRONG PLACE

One chilly morning in January, a man sat in a subway station in Washington DC and played the violin for 45 minutes. Approximately 1,000 people passed by during that time: Six of them paused for a few seconds and 20 people were moved to "drop some money into the hat".

A few days earlier, this same man, the violin virtuoso Joshua Bell, had performed to a full house in Boston where the seats averaged $100. On both occasions, he had played the same violin with an estimated value of $3,500,000, and the same Bach composition.

Bell played his violin in a 'less salubrious venue' in Washington DC but he remained confident in his ability as a musician, and he was still aware that he was one of the world's foremost violinists. Nevertheless, his "public" had not been able to grasp that – with him being in the wrong context.

THERE IS ALWAYS A CONTEXT

We constantly compare potential partners, services, and products of every description. Leaving someone, for example, often proves "easier" if we have met someone new against whom we can measure our current partner. Otherwise, we find ourselves in a very uneasy, "I know what I've got now, but not what might happen" situation, which we seek to avoid at all cost. We dislike uncertainty, and always want to know what's ahead – to be as sure as we possibly can be.

If we're contemplating doing business of some kind or buying a service, we start looking for relevant offers; very rarely, if ever, do we respond to the first offer we come across, even if it appears to be very, very attractive. Instead, we hold off until we've collated a few offers, or often a large number of offers, in order to make a reasonably informed comparison.

Frequently, however, the offers are frustratingly alike, and what decides our choice in the end is a feeling that something is somewhat better, somewhat less costly or we settle on something that feels in between.

In retail sales, businesses have long valued this knowledge, knowledge about how potential customers function – how we function.

I'm sure we can all remember having checked out, for example, a sweater costing $99.95 and (with good reason) thought it sounded a bit pricey. And on the very next hanger, a sweater originally priced at $150, now reduced to – you guessed it! – $99.95.

And suddenly, with this one, you're thinking "this is a really good buy!" How is this turnaround possible?

Such creative pricing, tends to work well on most of us, because it helps us find a reference point from which to base our actions; something to assure us we've done rather well – perhaps criminally well!

In short, we've based or anchored our judgment on the crossed out, but still legible, original price of the second sweater. This phenomenon is called the *anchoring effect*. Hey presto! The garment appears almost cheap when you consider its original tag price; although, ok, it's still expensive – especially as we had no intention of buying it at all after our first, uninformed appraisal.

An invitation to buy "three for the price of two" or "buy one, get one free" triggers a seemingly inherent instinct to buy something we had no intention of purchasing previously, to the extent that we completely forget to check what the usual list price is.

And then there's the classic "maximum three items per household". These deals are a cause of anguish if we learn about them after the fact. Ideally, we would have snapped up six – or more! Then we would have enjoyed the exhilarating feeling of having outsmarted the store.

In other words, many of the decision situations in which we find ourselves are already designed for us; tailor-made, as it were, for us to make the "right" decision as easily and quickly as possible.

It's as though someone up there were looking after us, someone who wanted us to make good decisions without too much agonizing or bother – someone who is willing to help us over the obstacles of buying a particular object or service.

IRRELEVANT INFORMATION IS RELEVANT

In a research study, an examination was conducted into how people choose, from the various options available, to buy subscriptions to *The Economist*. The alternatives presented were as follows:

I.   One-year subscription to the online edition, US $59

II.   One-year subscription to the print edition, US $125

III.   One-year subscription to the print and online editions, US $125

16% of the participants chose alternative I (online edition for $59). No one chose alternative II (print edition for $125); all the remaining participants, an overwhelming 84%, chose alternative III, offering both print and online editions for $125.

"Fair enough," is what of most of us are probably thinking, "it strikes me as a reasonable, logical outcome." But why was the middle alternative there in the first place?' Why indeed? In the study's second phase, alternative II (which clearly appears ridiculous; who would choose to get half as much for the same money?) was omitted.

I.   One-year subscription to the online edition, US $59

II. ~~One-year subscription to the print edition, US $125~~

III. One-year subscription to the print and online editions, US $125

Without alternative II, interest in option I significantly increased, with 68% of participants now choosing it. Conversely, alternative III, which had been the overwhelming favorite, lost 52% of its buyers.

To summarize: the "irrelevant and moronic" alternative II played a very big role in participants' eventual choice – despite everyone rejecting it. As this study confirmed, such irrelevant-seeming alternatives can quite easily lead us astray if we are not alert.

We rarely choose things in absolute terms. We have no innate ability to decide the value of things, for example, whether a particular table is worth $1,000. Instead, we consider the relative advantages of one item over another; we compare the table to other tables with similar attributes to work out whether it is worth its price.

For this reason, people engaged in making presentations at all levels should be clear when presenting information. They should avoid providing too much and, above all, imparting information that is not directly relevant and necessary. Otherwise, there is a risk that our audience focuses on the "wrong" things.

FIRST IMPRESSIONS LAST

Regarding the less than impressive (all too human) performance of the participants in the previous section, their choice could be defended by pointing out that no one issued the warning, "buyer beware" or suggested they should disregard misleading information.

What would have happened had these people been shown the type of information that is irrelevant to making a cogent decision and thereafter instructed them to TOTALLY disregard this information? Could they have then been expected to carry out the task as though they had never been warned? The answer is "no".

This could have been disregarded as much as we can stop thinking about a pink elephant, after having been firmly instructed to cease thinking about it.

That's how it is. So now, while you're thinking about the pink elephant, let us take a closer look at what happened when people were asked to guess what percentage of the African nations were members of the UN.

The participants were split into two groups, and before they were asked to make their guesses, a wheel of fortune was spun. The wheel was numbered 0 to 100, but rigged to always land on 10 or 65 depending on the group.

Group 1: When the wheel was spun for the people in this group, its arrow came to stop on 10. At this point, the participants were told: "As you can see, the wheel could have landed on any number. It stopped on 10 by pure chance and this result has absolutely nothing to do with reality. However, now that we have a number (10), let me ask you this, do you believe that the percentage of countries is higher or lower than 10%?" Next, they were asked to estimate what they thought was the actual percentage.

The calculated average of group 1's individual estimates came to 25%.

Group 2: When the wheel was spun for the people in group 2, it landed on the number 65. And they were duly given the same information as the people from the first group about this number's irrelevance and were asked the same closing question, but with the arrow pointing at the number 65: "Do you believe that the total number of member nations is more or less than 65%? Thereafter, they submitted their estimates.

The calculated average of group 2's individual estimations came to 45%.

The correct answer was 35%.

The interesting thing here is that the test subjects were not able to dismiss the "randomly" generated (irrelevant) number they had first been shown, but kept it in mind when making their guess. The number 10 (for group 1) and the number 65 (for group 2) influenced them far more than expected.

Thus, it was demonstrated that their guesses were significantly anchored to the first number they were shown. Although the number was irrelevant, it was something concrete, from which to work with, and when participants adjusted their estimates, they couldn't avoid the anchor.

In another experiment, people were given just enough time to glance at two different sets of multiplications that were displayed, as follows:

The first number series: 1x 2 x 3 x 4 x 5 x 6 x 7 x 8

The second number series: 8 x 7 x 6 x 5 x 4 x 3 x 2 x 1

The average guess for the answer to the first number series was 512.

The average guess for the second number series was 2,250.

Thus, the estimate, or guess, made for the series beginning with the lowest number (in this case, with the number 1 in the first series versus number 8 in the second) was significantly lower than for the second one. This is despite the fact that the actual calculation (40,320) is identical for both series.

HEY MONKEY, WHAT ARE YOU DOING AND WHY?

Cultural context steers decision making in businesses and organizations more than any strategy document, vision or decision support system ever will. Seldom, however, do we hear about this. We spend a shamefully meagre amount of time discussing culture's significance and focus far too little effort on that track. Many see culture as too light, soft and unimportant.

A long time ago, five cute monkeys were placed in a cage with a bunch of bananas set on the top of a ladder. Monkeys are, recognizably, very keen on bananas.

As predicted, one of the monkeys immediately raced towards the ladder to grab a banana. However, it was sprayed with ice-cold water. This happened every time a monkey tried to climb the ladder to grab a banana. But here's the thing – when one monkey went to grab a banana, the other four monkeys were also sprayed. The monkeys quickly learned their lesson – trying to climb the ladder equaled ice-cold water for everyone. As time went by, the monkeys were replaced one by one until none of the original monkeys remained, and the group's collective memory, naturally enough, began to waver. Yet, even though the cold water spraying had not been repeated with the new monkeys, the behaviour remained. Every time a new, happy, hungry and banana-lusting monkey arrived and rushed towards the ladder intent on retrieving the bananas, the other monkeys would go... bananas. They would quickly jump on the new arrival and let him know that he couldn't climb the ladder.

"Oh, really! Why not?"

"Well, we don't know, but that's the way we do things around here. Case closed."

In this way, it was made clear that a strong culture had been created. Everyone knew what he or she could and could not do – but no one knew why. Culture blindness in the majority of businesses is detrimental to decision making. Everyone does as they have always done, without bothering to reflect on whether what they're doing is good or bad.

In one of our research articles, *Managerial Decision Making under Risk and Uncertainty*, a high-level executive within the Swedish forestry industry put his finger on this phenomenon with strong conviction, stating:

"Here, we make decisions that correspond to 'Big Daddy's' will, otherwise you get another job."

The executive in question wasn't referring to his biological father, but to the boss above him. In the study, it was abundantly clear that the culture demanded that you accepted the status quo regarding how to think, act and decide. "Be happy with the situation" was the leitmotiv of the day, 365 days a year.

The majority of the leaders involved in the study explicitly stated that they too often did things as they had always been done; that they simply didn't dare to challenge the heavily entrenched culture, which in their own words, " ... was built into the walls."

HOW WE CHOOSE TO COMPARE

To a great extent, being free and happy is about being able to choose – true?

Free to choose how we want to live, where we want to live, what we want to eat, where we want to travel, who we want to live with, what we want to study, what interests we want to nurture, who we want to hang out with, what clubs we want to join, what make of cars we want to cruise in, and what clothing we want to be clad in – to name but a few of the choices we make.

For example, in Sweden there are more than 100 different electricity retailers, offering in excess of 3,000 different contracts. There are more than 800 "premium" pension funds from which to choose. The nation's colleges and universities offer more than 10,000 courses. There are 1,000 plus varieties of beer from which to choose. In the average large food emporium 30-40 different kinds of marmalade and jam can be found. It is likely that the spectrum of choice is even wider in other developed countries that are bigger than Sweden, which most are.

If the extent of freedom were to be measured in terms of opportunities from which to choose, we should, hands down, be far freer – and hence far happier – than ever before in the history of mankind. But are we, and with whom are we comparing ourselves?

Are rich people happier than the poor?

There is a certain correlation between happiness with life and income, but it is far from the direct "every dollar brings evermore delight" relationship, which we have been duped into believing. It has been shown that our overall happiness does not increase with rising incomes beyond the level where we have sufficient income to live well, without undue financial worry. Most of us understand this in a general sense, it is not that complicated.

What is quite surprising, however, is that those we believe would be as happy as it is possible to be, those who have won an extraordinary sum of money on the lottery or through other forms of gambling, ultimately end up less happy than people in general. Those who have won a great deal of money often base their personal concept of happiness on the rush they felt when the reality of their win first sank in. The winning ticket often turns out to be a very disillusioning booby prize, where many winners later find it difficult to appreciate life in its simplicity. That's one thing.

The other is that those who have periodically been really down-and-out in their lives – and have somehow managed to pull themselves up and out of this – are astonishingly, as it turns out, often happier than people in general. The many times they have experienced the downside of life first-hand and have made this their reference point (in sharp contrast to the "rush" reference of many one-time-only big winners). They don't take as much for granted and they appreciate life to a significantly higher degree than do people in general. Such people have become humble and gentle, they go wherever fate decides to take them.

Making comparisons helps us to make decisions in life, but this practice can also make us deeply despondent and unhappy. Why? Because jealousy often raises its destructive head when we compare our lot in life with that of others. Too often in life we wind up blindly fixated on what others have and what we do not. Happiness varies according to whom and what you compare yourself.

In Ari's parents' house there was a hung tapestry that read:

"If you wish to be cheerful and happy then remember this golden rule: miss not what is not there but relish the things that are."

Perhaps it's as simple as: our happiness does not depend on the conditions of life in which we have been placed, but by how they are embraced.

WHO IS RIGHT AND WHO IS WRONG?

The now legendary and highly celebrated Czech creator and filmmaker, Jan Svankmajer, exemplified the fact that it is not always easy, or simple, to answer the question posed above. In 1975, the communists banned his collection of work, whereas today, this collection is praised to the heavens.

What is righteous and right, here and now, can be condemned as decadent and wrong in the future – and vice versa. Who decides – those who were right in the past or those who are right today?

Over time, our perspective often changes. Forming our own independent perspective is a great strength – daring to stand for them is even stronger.

We must dare to believe in ourselves, especially when we think and act in ways that others do not – regardless of what others think or the price.

THE DIFFERENCE BETWEEN WHO YOU ARE AND WHO YOU WANT TO BE LIES IN WHAT YOU DECIDE TO DO.

SUMMARIZING TIPS

- Examine sale offers critically, with a degree of scepticism. When considering "middle way" alternatives and attention-grabbing offers, such as, "two for the price of one" or "as long as the supplies last", remember that the only purpose is to get us to buy more than we were planning to buy. Always reflect on WHY certain alternatives are tempting: is it because of the heavy discount or would you still have chosen it?

- Beware of "culture-blindness" and be wary of "facts", along with informal "regulations" and cultural behaviour codes, when decisions are to be made. Remember that behavioural changes cannot be accomplished overnight. Do not give up.

- When you make comparisons, try to disregard information or options that are not relevant to the evaluation being made.

- Be aware of the context in which information is being evaluated and/or the organizational context in which the decision is made.

- Be sure to keep your expectations realistic, in your professional life as well as life in general. It is absolutely crucial for your perception of yourself as either successful and happy or less content with life.

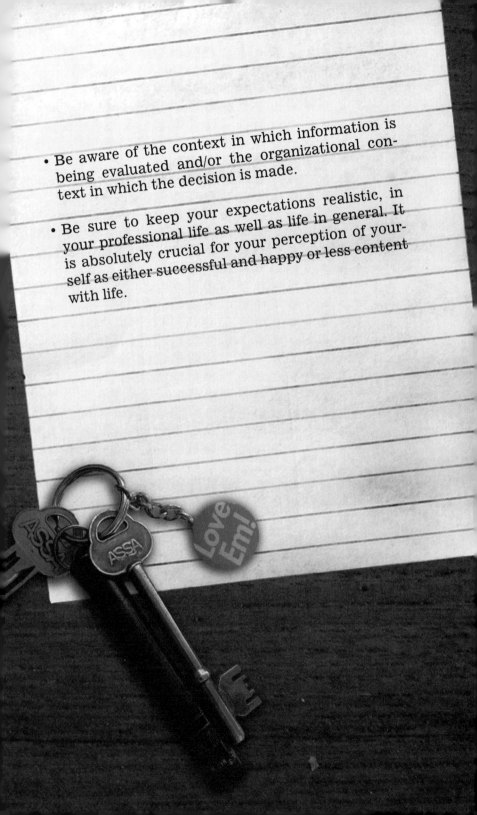

Step 4 of the Pyramid of Decision Making

INFORMATION

"Now that I've received
all the information,
I just want to
understand what the
hell it's all about?"

Henrik Tikkanen

THE MORE
THE BETTER?

John Stuart Mill, social commentator, author and philosopher, is said to have been the last man on this planet who knew all that was worth knowing.

He died 139 years ago.

We live in an age in which half of all available information is no more than 10 to 12 years old, and where new waves of information roll in at an ever faster pace. Gartner's 2013 technology trends found that digitally stored information was increasing at the rate of 59% per year, and we strongly suspect that this estimate hasn't decreased today. This means that a great many businesses are more than doubling the volume of their stored data – every two years. Within some scientific areas it is calculated that the volume of knowledge doubles every seven to eight years.

Often, we confuse additional information with increased knowledge, which is not necessarily the same thing – far from it, unfortunately.

INFORMATION

However, we have a natural protection mechanism, a mental filter, against all the impressions to which we are subjected. This filters out, among other things, the multitude of information that reaches our conscious mind. Instead, this is handled by our subconscious.

Despite this mental filter, it has become, and will continue to become, harder and harder to choose just the right bits information to digest and act on. The increase of information, within an already mind-boggling supply, is breathtaking and unrelenting. We will never be able to capture the big picture fully or analyse every detail.

This is a challenge we increasingly encounter because what constitutes today's complicated reality will not be the make up of reality a week from now, or perhaps even tomorrow. Reality alters too much, too fast, and at times too furiously, for us to grasp it completely. However, by analysing only small parts of reality, we may draw some unexpected conclusions.

Thinking about all of this reminded us of an episode from the 1960s when the controversial rock legend, Frank Zappa, was interviewed on American TV by (the then infamous) talk show host Joe Pyne. This was at a time when very long hair on men was still uncommon and controversial. Joe, who had a prosthetic leg fitted after an amputation, began the interview by remarking:

"I guess your long hair makes you a girl."

Zappa calmly snapped back with a memorably droll response:

"I guess your wooden leg makes you a table."

The tempo of modern society demands that we make use of shortcuts. Regardless of the type of decision we face, we will never be able to grasp all the alternatives fully – nor all the information we have gathered – no matter how much we want to.

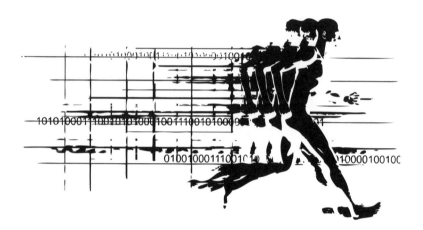

"Even in a chaotic world, some sense of stability can exist. While chaos does require you to act, it does not require precision."

J. Gutsche

GRASP THE CONCEPT

In order to make the right decision at the right time, we often require more than information. A vital key to better decision making is acquiring knowledge about how we can better identify information that is vital to the matter at hand; how we transform information into knowledge. This can pose problems, as knowledge is not always the thing we are looking for.

We live in a world that is fit-to-burst with information. It's as though we've become so totally captivated by information that we've begun to care less and less about knowledge. Just the word "information", in and of itself, has become reassuring. How important a supposed "wealth" of information might be is not considered so vital.

So, with this in mind, let's take a closer look at the concepts of *data, information and knowledge* – and thereby – hopefully gain a better understanding of how and when one concept merges into another. We have chosen to define them as follows:

Data and information are often equated with each other. Data can be everything from various facts, statistics, or some other type of "input" that, without processing, has little, or at best, marginal, value.

Basing a decision on raw data is not a preferred course of action. It generally leads to erroneous decisions since it tends to produce sweeping generalities which are not specifically designed for, or relevant to, the actual situation at hand.

Information, in turn, is often equated with knowledge. Information is data that has been manipulated into some form of completeness, processed to be relevant to a given context, which opens up the possibility of an "adapted" situation analysis.

Knowledge is the highest level and is obtained when information, which has been processed to the point where its relevance, intelligibility, and authenticity or functionality, have been established. It has at last been made precise and meaningful through analysis.

Decisions that are made intuitively or based purely on data, can often be made faster, but also contain a higher level of risk. The risk involved decreases the higher you climb in the concept hierarchy, and thus, basing decisions on knowledge is the least risky option – unless you need to decide very fast. #paradox

WE SEE WHAT WE WANT TO SEE

Often, when we look for information related to life in general, or in connection with our professions or workplaces, we see only the things we want to see – the things that benefit our aims.

We can carry this tendency so far that we'll keep on searching for information, until we find something that reinforces what we already know. Naturally we want enough to unearth information that supports our aim or standpoint. This phenomenon is called *confirmation bias*. This can occur both consciously and unconsciously, which is why it is especially important to focus serious thoughts around the sources being used. Are they reliable? Is the information being selected precisely the sort of information we like to hear – or that someone else has advised us to look out for? Or is it, indeed, the truth, the whole truth and nothing but truth, uncensored and unchained? Many times, the answer is somewhere in between.

We also tend to rely more on information from our boss than from our colleagues in an organizational setting. From an evolutionary and historic perspective, listening to our leader has helped us to survive. We also have a strong tendency to place more confidence in information for which we've paid than free advice – regardless of the actual quality of the advice from either source. We see daily proof of this in the consulting world, where clients tend to rely significantly more on expensive, rather than inexpensive, consulting firms. So, if you're looking to have people take your good advice seriously, then make sure they pay generously for your services.

But getting back to our tendency to search for the "right" information, in other words, the information we want to see. It's a tendency that makes us vulnerable in several ways. Quite simply, it prevents us from discovering things we hadn't given thought to or expected to see. This hindrance to discovery is called *inattentional blindness.*

Expectations about what we're going to find can make us blind to the obvious. An experiment that confirms this connection began with people arriving at a casino being required to fill out a form before they could begin playing. The man behind the reception desk welcomed the new arrivals, and after exchanging a few words by way of an introduction, he bent below the desk to fetch a pen (necessary for filling out the form). While he was momentarily out of sight behind the desk, he was replaced by another man who had been hiding there waiting for this moment. The casino guests never noticed the switch and continued chatting with the new man behind the desk as though nothing had happened.

INFORMATION

This was the case, despite all of the attendees having already conversed with the first man, and the notable fact that his "secret" replacement wasn't even similarly attired. Naturally, this group had no expectation of a person switch taking place on their arrival at the casino, hence its rather surprising success.

There is a great deal we don't expect to see – and much of what the future brings, we will have never seen before.

We should always listen skeptically when someone tells us to hold only to the truth and only to present objective facts. What is held to be objective has been proven to be subjective.

On one occasion, a chief executive told us that, at his company, managers were 100% objective when it came to interpreting the objective data that was collected in their KPIs (Key Performance Indicators) from which they directed the course of the business.

"Who has chosen the KPIs?" we wondered.

"I did," said the CEO.

So much for objectivity, as in so many cases.

INFORMATION GAP

TEST:

1) If you participate in a running event and pass the person who's running in second place, what place are you in?

2) Which of the following English expressions is correct? "The yolk of the egg is white" or "The yolk of the egg are white?"

Many would agree that spontaneous answers easily pop quickly to mind, answers that are sometimes all too quick.

A surprising number of people instantaneously deduce that if I've passed second, I must be in first – and answer accordingly; which, of course, is not the case: you've over-taken second and are now the runner in closest pursuit of the leader.

The example of the egg yolk helps us understand what happens when we don't have all the vital bits of information in mind. Most of us are so intensively focused on choosing the right verb form (*is* white versus *are* white) that we miss the question's overriding fundamental misstatement, which you have no doubt already discerned: the yolk of an egg – whether we are speaking of one or of many – is yellow.

Our brains do not like being subjected to information gaps and are therefore quick to fill them with the best ready answer or solution, without considering the situation in its entirety. We all have a fast track to interpreting what we see.

Our brains are skilled at pattern recognition and associating pieces of visual information with what we already know. Throughout history, this has helped us to make simplifying connections, which are often beneficial. At the same time, this process can be misleading if there is no relationship, context, or connection that helps us understand an unfamiliar event or piece of information. In such situations, the brain creates one for us – so we can make sense of it nevertheless.

STEREOTYPICAL

All aspects of decision making are affected by our way of simplifying, for example, the way we evaluate someone's performance, or decide on who we are going to employ. Everywhere and throughout society we routinely make judgments about people – about what they do, say and how they look – based on stereotypes.

Decision makers are generally unaware of how stereotypes influence their judgments, or even worse, that this problem exists in the first place.

Researchers consider that even as children we are already accumulating biases and creating stereotypes. Three-year-olds are already registering racist undertones with no understanding of their significance or meaning beyond the general "this good – this bad" impressions they are being fed. Most children accumulate a whole register of biases with regard to language, jokes and, tragically enough, discrimination – early on.

Once we have digested them, the stereotypes and biases we then hold steadfastly resist change, even when the information to which we're exposed to does not support what we've learned; even when such information clearly punches huge holes in their validity. People are receptive to anecdotes that support their biases, but easily disregard any facts and experiences that undermine them.

INFORMATION

A friend of ours, who happens to be Black and also quite large in size, once told us that people who approach him on the sidewalk late at night often cross the street.

Here in Sweden, it has to be said, people whose name and/or appearance differs from the Swedish norm, experience our society very differently from the majority.

Research reveals that although we may actively work at trying to free ourselves of biases, we cannot shed them entirely. They respond by hiding themselves more and more effectively in our subconscious, and from these remote havens still make their presence felt, especially when we are stressed, distraught, inebriated or competing.

Decision makers tend to rely less on stereotypes when they have sufficient information, time and motivation to devote to their decision making.

A classic experiment, conducted by Tversky and Kahneman, focused on how we react to representations of stereotypes, describing a fictional character, Linda, as follows:

Linda is 31 years old, single, outspoken, and very bright. She majored in philosophy. As a student, she was deeply concerned with issues of discrimination and social justice, and also participated in anti-nuclear demonstrations.

In the 1980s, many of the experiment participants in the US smiled. They immediately "knew" that Linda had attended the University of California, Berkeley, which was then renowned for its politically engaged students.

This fictional description of Linda further influenced most of the participants to consider it more probable that Linda worked in a bookshop and practised yoga than that she worked in a bank.

People also thought it more probable that Linda was a feminist who worked in a bank than simply a person who worked in a bank.

Clearly, the probability of her being a feminist who works in a bank, so both a feminist and a bank worker, is not greater than her being just a bank worker.

The probability of two events occurring together is always less than or equal to the probability of either one occurring alone.

A closely related phenomenon that also results in erroneous probability estimates is called *the accessibility heuristic*. This can cause us to over-estimate the probability of something occurring if a similar "something" recently took place. Therefore, an event, crisis, remarkable success, or so on, that is accessible in our memory bank appears to make its recurrence more probable to us. Many people, for example, felt it was more probable that a passenger airplane would be hijacked specifically by terrorists, than by another person or persons, for a long period of time following the catastrophic 9/11 hijackings in the US.

This mental phenomenon can also work to affect us in positive ways, for example, to increase/improve our performance. Referred to as 'priming' by psychologists, this describes the influence that recently digested/processed information can have on our subsequent short-term behaviour or performance.

Recalling a recent successful sale shortly before an important sales meeting is a practical, and oft-used, example of priming; reading an article about promising new techniques to increase physical endurance, the night before a heavy training session, is another. Less positive alternatives would be to fret over a sales campaign that went down the tubes, or to read about heart conditions that can be triggered by exercising.

So, it is important to remember that the newest information, regardless of its quality, to a very great extent tends to overshadow, or supersede, the information that came before it.

HALF AS MUCH IS TWICE AS GOOD

In 1956, the psychologist George A Miller published one of the 20th century's most widely read scientific works, *The Magical Number Seven, Plus or Minus Two: some boundaries to our ability to process information.*

According to Miller, in our short-term memory, which we can call "working-memory" (like the one in your computer), we can retain seven pieces of information; more specifically, we can remember, for example, seven numbers, or letters in the alphabet, for 30 seconds. These boundaries apply to information that lacks a context. As soon as information is set in a context, it becomes easier to remember (for longer and in greater quantities). For example, it is easier to remember that someone is a baker, than it is to remember that the same person's surname is Baker. Trained minds that compete in memory championships expand the memory bank further by using visual images to represent the abstract pieces of information, putting them in a context.

And when it comes to letters of the alphabet and numbers being combined, as with access codes on the internet, we find the performance of our memories significantly improves by clumping, so that the information comes out looking like this for example: CIA2015 or KGB1967, rather than just letting numbers and letters run together, unstructured.

Today, many assert that Miller was slightly too positive, or shall we say, generous, when it came to setting his boundaries, and that perhaps a more realistic magical number would read: five plus or minus two.

Our big challenge is to couple working memory with long-term memory. It is the latter that safely contains all our knowledge, all our experience and, to simplify it somewhat, our intuitive skills. You could say that long-term memory and short-term memory must meet – must have a dialogue – and that the bottleneck rests in the working memory's capacity. When the information is readily accessible then we get too much: our working memory simply cannot handle the load – our brains become flooded with information and we become stressed.

At the onset of stress, the brain's capacity to handle incoming information weakens. A stressed brain becomes easily tired and this sets our emotional system in motion. Our primal brain has an easier time perceiving something as a threat, and a stressed and frightened brain is quick to draw hasty conclusions, and therefore make inferior decisions.

Our brains would be at their very best if we received information like a glass catching drops under a leaky faucet ... ***drip-by-drip*** ... one soft drop at a time.

But instead, we experience the opposite, every day, year in, year out. Information does not reach our consciousness a drop at a time, it bursts forth like the volcanic gush of water from a fire extinguisher.

We are swamped with information, not least from the internet. Information has become inexpensive and readily accessible. Being able to evaluate information is no mean challenge. Is it a first-hand, second-hand, third-hand – or umpteenth-hand – source we've just accessed?

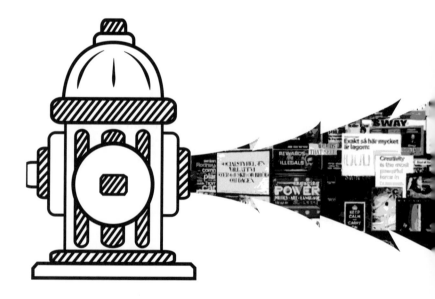

THE ANSWER LIES IN THE QUESTION

In a study, subjects were told that health officials were preparing for an outbreak of Asian flu expected to kill 600 people. Subjects were presented with one of two public health scenarios, where they had to choose between two plans (I or II) to combat the outbreak.

Scenario 1.

I.   If you choose vaccine A, 400 people will survive

II. If you choose vaccine B, then there is a two-thirds chance everyone will survive, and a corresponding one third risk that everyone will die

82% CHOSE VACCINE A

Scenario 2.

I.   If you choose vaccine A, 200 people will die

II.   If you choose vaccine B, then there is a two-thirds chance that everyone will survive, and a corresponding one third risk that everyone will die

ONLY 22% CHOSE VACCINE A

Despite the plans in the scenarios being mathematically identical, you and I may well react differently depending on which scenario we face. When presented with scenario 1, people are triggered by the word "survive" appearing in the first plan, whereas people presented with scenario 2 are scared off by the very "same" option due to the word "die".

This is called *framing* and it is an art that affects how we perceive and interpret information. In general, risks loom larger than potential gains, and thus the fear of losing something motivates people more than the prospect of gaining something of equal value. Therefore, framing the same situation in a loss frame has more effect than presenting it as a gain. With knowledge of how to frame (less formally: tweak) the same information to achieve different ends, or appeal to different interests, we can manipulate people into choosing or acting in different ways. Or we can be duped by how others present us with information.

Presenting information in a neutral manner is an art in itself – providing it's possible.

Many decision scenarios in which we find ourselves on a daily basis are constructed in a way that encourages us to choose a specific alternative, easily and intuitively – often a "middle" alternative; or a "preferred" alternative, as in the flu outbreak study.

Let's take a look at another research example in which people were asked whether or not they wanted to participate in an organ donation programme.

When the Swedish subjects were asked whether they were willing to donate their organs to medicine after death, most answered, "yes".

Look at the bar graph below to see how subjects from some other European countries answered. We don't need to be experienced analysts to notice that there are dramatic differences between countries that are pretty similar to one another in general terms, for example, Germany and Austria, or Sweden and Denmark.

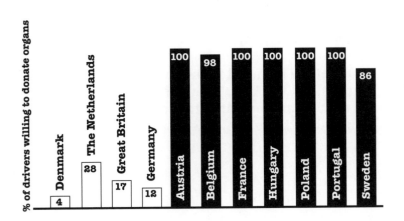

True, there are cultural differences between these countries, but from a general perspective, there are considerably more similarities than differences. And yet, the responses are so different with respect to theoretical willingness to donate organs. How is this possible?

The answer lies in the way the question was framed.

Nations represented by black bars were asked:
*Tick the box if you **don't want to** participate in an organ donation programme.*

Nations represented by white bars were asked:
*Tick the box if you **want to** participate in an organ donation programme.*

Regardless of how the question was formulated, the people responding thought along these lines: "No, this is too big a decision to decide here and now – I'll leave it as is."

It has been shown that it is significantly easier to allow the original, pristine situation to remain as is, than to change it actively.

Thus people behaved in the same way: only a few of them ticked the box. They reacted identically, and the result was calculated in record time – it too was identical, although reversed.

SCREW LOGIC, TELL A STORY

Only a few of us can handle letters and numbers with ease. This is because they are not natural for us. We remember relationships and contexts far easier than details and so-called, fully demonstrated presentations – regardless of how "sound" such presentations might be.

The following example is a so-called Wason Test. The test illustrates the largely unknown fact that we are neither fundamentally inclined, nor designed, to view things in an especially logical way; that is to say, with rigorously objective, deductive reasoning. We are far more suited to, and effective at, dealing with contexts.

Think of the following "playing" cards laid out on a table, and imagine that each card has a letter on one side and a number on the other. Which card or cards must you turn over to prove the following assertion right or wrong? *"Every card with a D on one side has a 3 on the other side."*

The overwhelming majority choose to turn the card with 3 showing. The right answer, however, is to turn the D-card and the card showing 7. The D-card proves the assertion is true, if it is true, and the card with the 7 on it proves the assertion is false, if indeed it is false.

Less than 25% of the students at Stamford University answered correctly when Leda Cosmides carried out the test at the university.

In his book, *Exploiting Chaos*, Jeremy Gutsche writes that the beautiful thing about the Wason Test is that you can ask the same question posed in an entirely different way.

Imagine you are working as a bartender and you have four customers, one of whom may be underage and therefore cannot be served beer.

Which of the four cards below do you need to examine more closely (turn over) to ensure you are not breaking the law by serving someone under the age of 18?

When the question was posed in this way (with directive words rather than a number or a letter) the total of right answers rose from a lowly 25% to a very respectable 75% – up a remarkable 50%, in other words.

Apparently then, it is easier for us to understand that the cards "drinking a beer" and "16 years old" must be turned, rather than the "D" and "7" cards in the first example.

When the question was posed in terms of a context, it became easier to understand and respond. We could perceive the situation better – it became more real to us. For better or worse, numbers are simply not "our thing".

Screw logic – tell a story!

CONSULT THE BRAIN BEFORE ENGAGING THE TONGUE

We must be explicit when informing others about something; for example, when giving a presentation. That is, if our aim is to enable others to arrive at an informed, intelligent decision/opinion about the matter being presented. And vital to achieving this end, and to informing related developments, is the way the information itself is presented.

Often, decisions are most influenced by how we put information across rather than by our presentation's substance.

An example of when these problems become unmistakably apparent is when we attend a conference – it could be of any description – and are subjected to PowerPoint bombardments.

Even before being compressed by PowerPoint, presentations often contain so much information that our listeners cannot keep up. Consequently, they often find themselves shell-shocked, in a state of suspended animation. They simply don't have the capacity to take it all in. The whole experience – paradoxically enough – often results in a pleasant day out of the office, but what do people remember – what do they take with them?

When we carry out a PowerPoint "carpet-bombing", we lose our audience. We have said all we feel the urge to say, which has proven to be rather a lot.

If you wish to be interesting – be interested. And say not what you want to say, say what people want to hear – say something that moves them.

The example of presentations and conferences gives an indication of the challenges we face when we communicate within businesses and organizations.

If we're not able to produce a couple of slides so that people can keep up, how can we communicate our goals and strategies to the troops all lined up and marching in the planned direction?

And how are we to pass on information successfully to people in the organization, to help them make better decisions?

INFOHOLICS ANONYMOUS

As we touched on earlier, we collect information because lots of detail makes us feel more certain of our position; but it seldom makes us better decision makers. However, this is a relatively small challenge.

The big challenge is that most of us have become addicted to information. We've become information junkies. And once we've developed a deep addiction, we invariably want more – no matter the drug in question. Our tolerance levels steadily rise, and information addiction is no exception.

In a nutshell: the brain's reward system reacts to information as it does to sex, sweets, shopping sprees or drugs, medicinal or otherwise. Information causes dopamine to flood our brains, and dopamine, among other things, can act as an arousal serum that puts us in a very good mood. In this way, it encourages us to seek to participate in a range of activities fundamental to human survival – sex, eating, competing and so on.

Most drug addicts have a favorite drug. By the same token, many people in today's information society have Excel as their favorite drug.

The dopamine flows when majestic bars and beautiful diagrams are displayed on our computer screens and on the far larger white screens that have become a must in conference rooms around the world. If the drug of choice is not at hand, surely option B will do almost as well: Facebook, Twitter or email, anyone?

The brain makes no distinction between the drugs to which it's exposed, whether they've been purchased on a shadowy street corner, prescribed by a doctor, or delivered to your door by a retail liquor chain outlet – it's all the same. This also applies to brand-spanking new information, whether in the form of an Excel spreadsheet, e-mail, or from a brief, casual surf on Facebook.

We fear, or more correctly, we hope and believe that, in the near future, we will see the organization INFOHOLICS ANONYMOUS begin to grow like flowers in spring. The need is already here, but the addiction is not yet fully recognized by the general public, and our lives are not yet totally unmanageable. Welcome – in due time.

SUMMARIZING TIPS

- When seeking information, in order to avoid seeing only the things we want to see, and hearing only what we want to hear – whether consciously or unconsciously – we must carefully consider the sources we're using and why.

- Try to differentiate data, information and knowledge – and use knowledge as the basis for making vital decisions.

- We should be wary of drawing conclusions based on only a small portion of (a given situation's) reality. Even if the information is correct, the conclusion can easily turn out to have been too hasty.

- Challenge yourself to be more critical in your thinking. Collect information from different sources; seek advice from different personality types; and try to access information that is unconsciously allowed to slip away by reinforcing the structure of your decision making. Checklists and other simple procedures are good ways to avoid missing vital details.

- Be aware of our tendency to judge people according to stereotypes and to overestimate the probability of something occurring if something similar recently took place. Make use of the fact that recently digested information can have a positive influence on our subsequent short-term behaviour or performance by "priming" your mind with suitable information.

- Be aware that the format and the presentation of information, known as framing, affect how it is received and how people make decisions. Halt the PowerPoint bombardments when giving presentations.

- We can retain five to seven items in our "working-memory" for about 20-30 seconds, and then it's gone. Don't forget that!

TECH

"If technology is
the answer, what
is the question?"

LYRICS FROM THE SWEDISH SYNTHPOP
BAND ADOPLPHSON & FALK:

FLASHING BLUE, 1981

THE CONTROL IS FLASHING BLUE,
A SIGNAL FOR THE SECURE,
THE CONTROL IS FLASHING BLUE,
THEN ALL IS WHAT IT SHOULD BE.
IF THE SCREEN IS NORMAL
THERE IS NO REASON TO DOUBT.
WHEN THE CONTROL IS FLASHING BLUE,
THEN ALL IS WHAT IT SHOULD BE.

BUT IN THE QUIET HOURS OF THE NIGHT
I'VE WONDERED WHAT HAPPENS WHEN
TECHNOLOGY DOESN'T SEE, WHAT'S HIDING
IN THE SHADOWS OF THE THUJA TREE.
AND MY CONCERNS GROW MORE AND MORE.

BUT THE CONTROL IS FLASHING BLUE...

BUT THERE ARE QUERIES THE COMPUTER
CANNOT ANSWER, SIGNALS THAT I CANNOT
UNDERSTAND. THERE ARE SO MANY THINGS
WE CANNOT EXPLAIN. THERE ARE FORCES WE
CANNOT INFLUENCE.

BUT THE CONTROL IS FLASHING BLUE...

COMPUTERIZED DECISION MAKING

When computers arrived on the scene, many thought that a solution to improving the decisions of fallible mankind was in sight. People had high hopes that, in the not too distant future, computers would be making decisions for us. And indeed, today we have fantastic technical resources at our disposal, particularly when it comes to processing massive volumes of data, many used in the decision making of businesses and organizations. A large proportion of the decision making carried out by businesses and organizations is computerized, but far from all; and more significantly far from all the most vital and difficult decisions. These often require another type of skill: manual tweaking.

A large part of the difficult decisions we make are unique. We rarely, or never, encounter them in exactly the same guise or format, which – for practical purposes – makes them impossible to standardize or automate.

Today, it's easy to access almost every category and type of data and process them at an ever lower cost. Hardware capacity and various computer tools created to aid decision making, so-called decision-support systems, are found in abundance. It should also be noted here that decision support is a broad concept, under whose umbrella can be found everything from calculation programmes, such as Excel, to advanced analytical programmes.

Many companies see analysis as a strategic instrument and employ analytical experts to discern patterns in data and forecast trends. Analysis can be used to customize special offers for customers based on what other customers, who bought the same products previously, had purchased. Or to put it into context: precisely the sort of offers the majority of adult Swedes receive on a weekly basis from ICA, Sweden's largest grocery and variety retail chain.

By analyzing what we have purchased previously, ICA can then offer us particularly "tempting" discounts to be cashed-in the next time we go grocery shopping.

Another example of the uses of data analysis is when credit card companies are able to predict divorcing customers, based on telltale changes in their buying habits. The reason this is of particular interest to credit card providers is that an alarmingly high-percentage of recent divorcees will have difficulty meeting their monthly payments.

Nowadays, businesses are not limited to making good use of their own computer-based information. As well as, for example, a categorized history of customer purchases, and the web links people have clicked, but also external data sources such as social media that provides access to information about buying trends, regarding travel, dining out, cultural interests, and so on.

It is said that 80% of the types of data we have today did not exist four years ago. This is another telling indication which suggests that we have only seen the initial phase of the possibilities of data analysis and it is but a fraction of the massive volumes of data awaiting us in the future.

In many areas we have become aware of the pressing need for data-based decision support and, in line with this need, the majority of businesses have happily invested in such support over recent years. In 2012, talk focused on mobile services, and the mystical "cloud" in which businesses were advised to store data or, conversely, not to. The trade press also reported that the global market for business intelligence was estimated to be worth more than $9 billion, steadily growing. Further development of the technology underlying this growth area is reportedly insensitive — to changes in the overall level of business activity. With the aid of this technology, for example, a business can boost its sales during "good times" – and during "bad times" a business can, with the help of this same technology, significantly reduce its costs.

During 2013, we read, time and again, that for most companies this was the year of big data, business intelligence and decision support – explaining the reason for this area's high position on the list of business investments. No one likes the prospect of lagging behind. We may not always know precisely what we want, and the same can be said about what we need – but we do know there is something we want, and likewise, we also know there is something we need.

But how is all this technology going to be used? Will it just be a matter of plugging it in, switching on the power and letting the systems do the rest? Many people believe that, and we wish it were so. Unfortunately, the results of efforts in this direction have thus far, time after time, made it clear that making this wish a reality is not that easy.

WE HAD A DREAM

When studying as PhD students, we had a dream, a dream about how effective decision-support solutions should be constructed – and most particularly – their underlying cornerstones. In the decision-support triangle, everything was woven together like the words and lines of Shakespeare's sonnets. Decision makers and organizations, goals and strategies, technology and information; each interdependent element contributed to the achievement of a common goal.

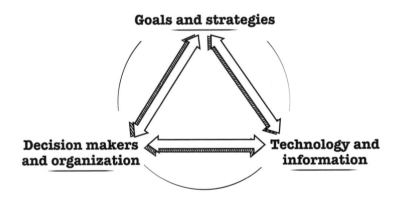

How we thought decision-support solutions should look

But when we left the university and entered the world of business, the picture did not look the same. Here, business intelligence, which is often viewed as synonymous and interchangeable with decision support, was mainly concerned with data warehouses/marts, cubes, ETL (Extract, Transform and Load) processes, reporting tools, and information, as far as the eye could see. In other words, business intelligence was mainly concerned with processes suited to technological support. It soon became apparent that it had very little to do with such business concerns as governance, the future, risk, or strategy. In fact, business intelligence had very little to do, relatively or absolutely with conducting intelligent business, period. Not to mention the total absence of deliberative focus on current decision processes; that is, the processes the technology was supposed to support. Nor was there a trace of such troublesome words as "people", "culture" or "decision makers".

Such lapses are serious for several reasons. If we lack knowledge about a company's current decision making processes (the applicable processes used to make decisions at every company level) then it is very difficult, if not impossible, to support and/or reinforce them. In short, we must know what we are supporting before we can say how to do it.

In the event that we don't know, then some simple, introductory questions need to be asked, questions such as: "How is your decision making functioning today? Where do you see a need for improvement, and what measures do you see as necessary to bring it up to par?" And last but not least, perhaps the most important question of them all "Which are the most important decisions for your business?"

Based on what we observed, it was evident that the research world's triangle had been heeled over towards technology and information. Given this imbalance, it's reasonable to ask why Picture Two looks the way it does. We see several reasons for this.

Goals and strategies

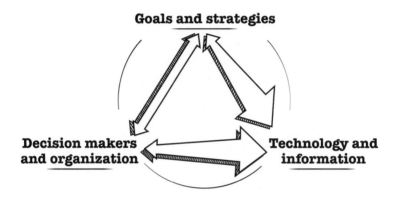

Decision makers and organization

Technology and information

What it actually looks like

I.   **Reason one** is that it is relatively easy to achieve something concrete by purchasing more technology. Likewise, the authority and influence of a report, is, more often than not, perceived directly proportional to the amount of information it contains. In both cases, it is abundantly clear that something has been done. Bravo! In fact, CEOs or other high-ranking executives have even been known to take credit, and not without some measure of justification, for having initiated a solution and seen to its implementation. This is probably the prime reason for businesses and organizations to, time after time, obstinately skip the decision pyramid's fundamental levels (people, herd animals and context) – to pole-vault to the pyramid's top – and solely focus on information and technology.

But one cannot rectify moving in the wrong direction by moving faster. Eventually, without knowledge of the decision pyramid's fundamental levels, there is an imminent risk that the entire structure will crumble.

II. **Reason two** is that when it comes to people, tangible results are significantly more diffuse and slower in coming, especially if it's been decided to look for decision making solutions elsewhere. In addition, particularly to businesses, there is the all-important matter of the bottom line. When we invest in technological solutions, these appear as an asset on the balance sheet. When we invest in the most valuable asset a company possesses, its people, this appears as a cost.

An interesting discussion between a CEO and his CFO (chief financial officer):

CFO:
What if we invest all this money in all these people and they leave the company –
then what?

CEO:
What if we don't invest all this money in all these people and they choose to stay –
then what?

III. **Reason three** is that often people tend to be working to a deadline when a decision-support solution is about to be implemented. And when we are stressed, it is much easier to think short term rather than long term. In such situations, we are often swayed by the possibility of finding a quick solution with the help of technology. Moreover, when we have a quick solution in sight, the pilot study invariably gets derailed. It is often conveniently summed up as " ... only costing a massive amount of money and taking up an unnecessary, massive amount of time from the project" (or words to that effect). This is naturally unfortunate, as a pilot study is unquestionably one of the most vital contributing factors to the success of a decision-support project, precisely as it is to so many other projects and connections.

Carrying out a decision-support project without first conducting a well-considered pilot study is much the same as writing an essay or dissertation without having defined your question, nor focus within its particular context; and perhaps most importantly, without having decided your explicit purpose. In short, it is extremely difficult, if not impossible.

Being careless with the pilot study and making too many experienced-based assumptions, inexorably leads to the creation of expensive solutions that fail to support the organization in an effective, definitive way. Thus, these tend to become solutions that are not used to the extent that had been hoped for and earnestly believed in.

WHAT'S IN IT FOR ME?

O nce upon a time, there was a company in, let's say, the field of insurance. At this company, one of the largest in Sweden, it had been determined, on very solid grounds, that a new CRM system (Customer Relations Management system) was needed. The general purpose of such systems is to provide better oversight of a business's customers and their needs. The primary aim of the company in question was to secure a system that was better able to "tailor" (individualize) insurance offers made over the phone. So far, so good.

A new system was specially designed and all that remained – four years and some 25 million Swedish krona ($3 million) later – was to roll out the system. In principle then, the only thing left to do was to "flick the switch". The problem was that there wasn't any "roll out the system" switch. Such a switch is yet to be invented.

It turned out that the targeted users of this new system were not primed or prepared for this arduous change, a journey about which they had been given minimal information. The system, nonetheless, was rolled out, to the extent it could be, a little here and there within the organization, and so-called pilot tests were duly made, but nowhere was the hoped for "improvement effect" reported.

For all those who had been involved in the project from its inception, and contributed their skills to the creation of the specially designed system's fine technical platform, its less-than-successful launch was a complete mystery.

"This is really strange," muttered one of the brains behind the solution. "It's an incomprehensible scandal that the users do not know what they're supposed to do. We have, as you're well aware, spoken to them once!"

In other words, he knew, or should have known, what the problem was. His team had spoken to all the users once only. However, getting users on board, establishing organizational backing and ensuring that system solutions significantly increase support to an organization in its business dealings and decision making, require getting the primary users involved, from the earliest stage. It involves keeping them on board continuously, right through to the journey's end and beyond.

The users and the so-called operational entity, whether applicable to a business or other organization, must be involved before, during and after a new system is developed, implemented and adopted. Otherwise, and this is guaranteed: it will not achieve the required results.

We often assume that others understand, agree or think in certain ways. We use ourselves as "the norm", and figure that what is important to us is also important to others. Instead of explaining, and being explicit (sometimes seemingly unnecessarily so), we make assumptions. However, we often need to communicate more, because "assumption is the trigger for future screw ups".

Those who decide, develop and implement systems must understand the weight carried in a question that is repeated like a mantra by people within the field of change management:

"What's in it for me?"

If you are a leader, you must exploit the thinking and concepts associated with individual profit or gain to be made by using the new system. The users must feel they are part of it and understand why it is in their best interests to use the system.

In general, for people (meaning you and I), to embrace something new, they must first truly understand the reason for doing so. Without this, we prefer to continue doing as we have always done. Therefore, it is vital to see that the aim and the value of introducing a new system is communicated "over and over again" in order to make sure the new system actually comes into productive use. It's essential to stress the importance of prioritizing communication when planning major changes, since we know there are often communication deficiencies in this connection, and that said deficiencies can be rectified with relatively little expense.

We must, in a very straightforward and obvious way, show that we grasp the difference between "user-friendly" and utilized systems, and that we are not content simply to present the former and leave it at that. Instead, we put more resources into the "entity" that steers the decision making process more than all others: the individual person, the decision maker.

The paradox of decision making

Investments

What governs decision making

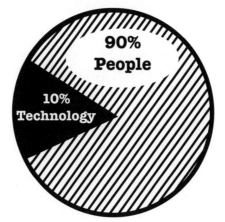

WE CAN IMPROVE

An article published in *Harvard Business Review* in 2010, reported the findings of a study in which it was stated that average business firms, " ... are way behind on decision making," compared with the leading firms.

On a scale of zero to 100, weighing the effectiveness of decisions made in businesses and other organizations, the average score of decision effectiveness in the study was calculated to be 28. The very best companies registered an impressive 71. We don't even dare to think of the worst decision effectiveness scores; would you?

Many businesses look over their marketing plans, goals and strategies, and processes of every sort. But few analyze how people make their decisions; how these decisions relate to, for example, goals and strategies and not least, how they could improve their decisions.

In an article we wrote that appeared in *CFO World*, we responded to the question of why businesses often fail to get more out of their investments in systems designed to provide decision support.

The answer is simple, today, more than 90% of the resources stocked in decision-support investment are found in the "technology box". There is nothing strange about that, it's the source of money for both (technological) providers as well as consulting firms.

"It's so wonderful having all these reports. Before, we had nothing, you see …", a phrase often heard after the report system has been installed.

Not long after, it often becomes apparent that too much information is being sent out – all the information that the client could conceivably be interested in having, without a great deal of precision and without having thought through how the information is to be used in the relevant operational decision making.

Despite the enormous potential that today's technological solutions offer, we know that businesses and organizations too often are getting way too little out of their investments, and often, the capacity they've acquired is being used in a deficient way.

In a study conducted with research colleagues at Stockholm University in 2011, approximately 50 Swedish companies were asked about their investment in business intelligence. The results of the study revealed, among other things, the following:

• According to 60% of those questioned, their business intelligence strategy was not well anchored, if at all, to the highest echelon of leadership.

• More than half thought that the business intelligence systems failed to deliver relevant information to the users in terms of business requirements.

- Half of the examined businesses had not established a business case before they invested in business intelligence.

- Half stated that information from the business intelligence systems was neither easy to understand, nor use.

- The great majority did not follow well-established routines when the organization and/or users were to be informed about, and prepared to use, new technology and information.

- Nearly 80% had poor, very poor, or no understanding whatsoever, of how new, accessible information could be used in existing decision processes.

- A total of 80% of the businesses had been wholly or partially unsuccessful in measuring the business advantage of business intelligence – if they had even made an attempt.

- According to 75% of the businesses, they lacked guidelines and procedures to explain and facilitate the way information from the business intelligence systems should be used.

- More than half of those questioned reported that they did not use even half of the information they derived from their business intelligence systems.

We must create solutions based on an entirety, the so-called "whole" – specifically; solutions where we have taken into account all the decision pyramid's steps. And we must create solutions where we begin by asking questions and working out procedures for definitively establishing:

what shall be done

who shall do it

when it shall be done (and so on)

Keep in mind that a mass of information is not going to make an unhappy person happy if we don't do something sensible with it. Not everyone should have access to all information, but everyone should have precisely the information he or she needs to be able to make better decisions.

**Information changes nothing,
Decisions change everything.**

HOW CAN
WE IMPROVE?

Most organizations need computer support in order to make better and quicker decisions in the complex and fast-changing world in which we live in, so far, so good. Unfortunately, far too often and far too quickly, the focus of decision support projects is on technological questions when seeking to improve the decision making performance. But decision making is a multifaceted process and the knowledge surrounding it embraces a great deal more than technical know-how and solutions, immensely more, in fact. Focusing solely on technology will lead to incomplete solutions at best.

Countless decision makers have expressed their unease, and even palpable discomfort, about the fact that regardless of what they ask about the answer is essentially the same: a new system, the upgrading of a dated one, or new reports you can "easily click to bring forth like this ..."

A decision question is often automatically reformed as a question concerning technology – a question that is hijacked by those who master the technology, and the overriding concept to which it belongs.

Before we go blind staring at technology's possibilities, it's vital to build a comprehensive perspective. A problem or fault cannot be rectified hastily. Instead, it is necessary to commit to penetrating beneath the surface and boring down to the root cause with an open mind and a fair number of vital questions.

We must, in other words, look at the big picture. Likewise, we must have an understanding of both the business-related and the organization-related pre-conditions, where the people working within the organization play a significant role. Thereafter, we can begin to contemplate if, and if so, how, the technology at hand can help us produce better pre-conditions for decision making.

When helping businesses and organizations through our company, we work on improving the effectiveness of their decision making and we usually begin by examining the current decision making and conducting a workshop. In turn, we bring up and analyze the pre-conditions and challenges in the areas (see flow illustration with post-its on the following page) that have the biggest effect on how decisions are actually being made. It requires a new mindset, an approach where the decision perspective is explicit, where more discipline is injected into how decisions are, and should be, made in order to achieve efficiency and prepare for better future decision making.

1. ORGANISATION & DECISION MAKER

MOTIVATION
LEADERSHIP
RULES
INDIVIDUALS
GROUPS
POLITICS
NORMS
DECISION PROCESSES
HIERARCHIES

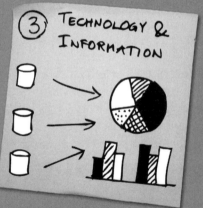

3. TECHNOLOGY & INFORMATION

2. GOALS & STRATEGIES

By beginning with the decision makers and the organization, it's possible to gain a good overview of the current decision processes, and roles in these, the decision culture that currently prevails, the type of information that is sought (and used), the norms, and the organization form (matrix, division, strict hierarchy and so on) in place. Taken together, this gives a good picture of the current situation, and points to those areas in which there is potential to bring about improvements.

Thereafter, when we review the standing goals and strategies, it is vital to identify which decisions within the business or organization are critical; the four or five decisions that have the strongest influence on the company's future. We must also acquire knowledge of how, and if, the existing decision making is working to support the efforts of the company's various departments to meet stated goals. Are decisions being made quickly enough? Is the right information being used? Are the risks the company takes in the course of business reasonably prudent and proportional? Has the company's leadership kept an eye on the future, or has decision making largely been a matter of quelling fires that suddenly spring up?

Not until we have come this far can we begin to evaluate the need for some form of technological support – and the technology or technologies best suited to the specific task in question.

Technical solutions must wait until we know the pre-conditions, as well as the other existing needs of the company.

What information do we need and for what purpose? What decisions are to be made and by whom?

How do you make decisions today? Fast, slow, like you always have, based on facts and knowledge or on instinct and experience?

Did you know that the culture steers the decision making more than any system in the whole world? What does your culture look like?

What do current decision processes look like and how is existing information to be used?

Which decisions are the most business critical in the next two, five or 10 years?

And perhaps the most important of all the questions: How do we ensure that we implement the decisions we make? Simply making decisions is not going to make an unhappy person happy if we don't follow them through.

The questions in the speech bubbles are issues that are addressed with too little time and too few resources in most decision-support projects. This is a shame. Because these are questions that must be answered in order to arrive at solutions that will be used and generate business advantages.

Ergo! Always be sceptical of someone who comes up with the right solution without having first asked the right questions.

As yet, the project is still not finished – because the process is cyclical in nature, and when development of the technological system solution is well underway, it is vital that earlier stages are not forgotten. The circle is continuously repeated during the development and implementation phases. Last, but not least, don't forget to provide the right resources for the things that steer decision making more than anything else: people and culture.

DON'T WE LIKE TECHNOLOGY?

But of course we like technology! We are, when all is said and done, a bit "nerdy", in addition to being Doctors of Philosophy in risk and decision analysis within computer and system sciences.

What we don't like, on the other hand, is the spectre of businesses and other organizations failing to gain even moderate benefit from the considerable investments they've made in all the technological systems available in today's business intelligence market. It's also one of the primary reasons we've written this book, in the hope that the people who read it will have more success.

Many people tend to make it unnecessarily hard for themselves by failing to take into account the fact that the hand on the control stick is attached to a human being – that it is people, just like us, who make up the ranks of so-called decision makers.

In order to make better decisions – sometimes with the help of technology – we must develop a greater understanding of, and insight into, how human beings function: why we do as we do, and choose as we do; the fact that we humans like to join with others and be a part of something, particularly when it comes to fixing or improving the environment in which we are going to perform, do business, and make decisions.

Let's not muddy the water. Use a little common sense, and don't come up with solutions without having first asked the right questions. Rely on us, and the chances are excellent that, however hard the decision problem, the solution will be found.

The saying goes: The simple is the ingenious. So, keep it simple!

Keep in mind the words of Swedish businessman Ingvar Kamprad, the legendary founder of international furniture emporium Ikea:

"It requires great competence and skill to work out simple solutions: Expensive solutions – for all types of problems – are most often signed by mediocre talents."

SUMMARIZING TIPS

- Much of today's decision support has enormous potential, but benefiting from its full effect requires directing focus on people – the decision makers.

- Be alert to the fact that at planning meetings focused on, let's say, installing a more effective business intelligence system, the discussions too often (and too quickly) focus almost exclusively on technological questions. All present forget the balance that must exist between goals and strategies, decision makers and organizations, alongside technology and information.

- Carry out an exhaustive pre-study before designing and implementing a decision-support system. Taking this measure is the alpha and omega of designing and implementing a system that will come to be used and create business opportunities.

- Ensure the business's current decision processes and the decision makers' role in them is apparent to everyone involved. How else can we even begin to support them?

- "What's in it for me?" The profit or gain to be made by using the new system must be made explicit to intended users and they must be involved throughout the phases of development and implementation.

- In order to make better decisions, we must acquire greater knowledge about the foundations of the decision pyramid – people and culture – and remember: the simple is the ingenious – keep it simple!

POSTSCRIPT

The inspiring memoir, *The Top Five Regrets of the Dying*, by Australian author Bronnie Ware, contains some interesting musings and details of enlightening conversations she's had with people during her work in palliative care. Over the years she spent tending to the needs of those who were dying, among the things she discussed with them was what they regretted most when they looked back on their lives.

Let us, as conclusion to this book, take a look at this special "what people regret most" list. Let us learn from it now, while we have a chance to change things, before it's too late. We still have the chance to make the biggest decision of all: how we choose to live the rest of our lives.

What people regret most at the end of their lives:

- "I wish I had been true to myself, instead of forming my life according to what others expected of me."

- "I wish I hadn't worked so hard."

- "I wish I had dared to express my feelings."

- "I wish I had kept in contact with my friends."

- "I wish I had allowed myself to be happier."